INSIDERS TALK
WINNING
WITH LOBBYISTS

INSIDERS TALK
WINNING
WITH LOBBYISTS

READERS EDITION

ROBERT L. GUYER

LOBBY SCHOOL

Engineering THE LAW, Inc.
13714 N. W. 21 Lane
Gainesville, Florida 32606, USA

Published 2018 by Engineering THE LAW, Inc.
Printed in the United States of America

20 19 18   1 2 3 4

ISBN 978-0-9677242-3-2
Library of Congress Control Number: 2018947554

Dedication

Oh the joy when the son surpasses the father,

dedicated to Benjamin M. Guyer, Ph.D.

TABLE OF CONTENTS FOR READERS EDITION

CHAPTER 1. OVERVIEW OF LOBBYING

CHAPTER 2. UNDERSTANDING CONTRACT LOBBYISTS

CHAPTER 3. UNDERSTANDING LAWMAKERS

CHAPTER 4. WHEN FACTS MATTER AND WHEN THEY DON'T

CHAPTER 5. POWER AND CORRUPTION

CHAPTER 6. ETHICS LAWS FOR LOBBYISTS AND CLIENTS

CHAPTER 7. CAMPAIGN CONTRIBUTIONS

CHAPTER 8. LOBBYING SPECIAL INTERESTS AND COALITIONS

CHAPTER 9. LOBBYING LEGISLATIVE STAFF

CHAPTER 10. LOBBYING EXECUTIVE AGENCIES

CHAPTER 11. LOBBYING LEGISLATORS

CHAPTER 12. LOBBYING THE GOVERNOR

CHAPTER 13. EXECUTIVE AGENCY RULEMAKING, APPEAL, AND ENFORCEMENT

PREFACE

Insiders Talk: Winning with Lobbyists Readers Edition overviews the lobbying process and roles played by lobbyists, clients, governors, lawmakers, agency staff, legislative staff, and special interests. Our *Professional Edition* goes into much greater detail showing *consumers* of lobbying services how to find and work effectively with contract lobbyists, negotiate better fees, manage their lobbying campaigns, and improve their chances of legislative success. The *Professional Edition* includes hiring documents and job performance evaluation instruments.

Whether from my own lobbying as in-house government affairs staff and as a contract lobbyist in both state and federal legislatures, from the thousands of lobbyists, both beginners and experts, who have participated in my *Lobby School,* and from the many contributors to this book, all the lessons and examples herein are real and applicable to anyone who works with contract lobbyists.

EXPECTED CRITICISMS

Critics may correctly point out they know specific exceptions to almost every one of my general observations. Others will accurately note I'm a lawyer and a lobbyist, not a political scientist, and some of my broad technical overviews as to formal processes and political understandings are deficient or inapplicable to their particular legislatures.

However, as to *lobbying practice*, this book is spot-on because it is based on the collective experiences of contract and in-house lobbyists and consumers of lobbying services. Our experiences include state, federal, and international advocacy. These consumers of lobbying services have hired hundreds of lobbyists at the U.S. state and federal levels.

ACKNOWLEDGMENTS

A book is seldom the work of one person. First, I want to thank the thousands of lobbyists who have attended my *Lobby School*. Approximately 70 percent of the anecdotes and lessons herein come from them and their experiences.

Next, I thank the dozens of lobbyists who each contributed a point, clarification, or a brief comment to this book. Finally, I especially want to thank those who reviewed the manuscript for their criticisms and suggestions. Several quotes herein come from *The Lobbying Handbook* by John L. Zorack.

Finally, I thank Katherine Lee Amy, my wife and greatest supporter, for her patience during the four years I spent writing this and other books. She calmly tolerated my preoccupation with writing, let me explore ideas with her, edited my dozens of drafts, and accepted the immediate financial losses that came from me writing rather than giving income producing *Lobby School* seminars. Being herself an extremely successful managed health care consultant, her experiences and insights with consulting in general contributed to key sections of the book.

ATTRIBUTIONS

As readers of this book must doubtless notice, two behaviors which are highly prized in the world of legislatures and lobbying are maintaining confidentiality and practicing trustworthiness. Clients, lobbyists, legislators, and government personnel may require certain conversations be kept private and must feel confident they can trust the person with whom they are speaking to uphold privacy. At the same time, however, those readers who want to understand the complexities and challenges of the lobbying world need to hear the voices of people intimately involved with the activities described in the following chapters.

Contributors provided valuable information but not at the price of their jobs. To illustrate, one reviewer observed, "I have forgotten what horrible confessions I made, but they are all true, and it is likely for the best that they not be attributed to me." A western states government affairs director wrote, "**Please do not directly cite my name on these ... some would get me into some hot water.**" (Emphasis in original) A mid-Atlantic in-house lobbyist after considering the potential impact his candor could have on his career concluded, "After much thought, I'd say let's stay with anonymous." For that reason, this book contains a number of direct quotations which do not have full attribution (specifically, name of speaker) typically required in situations where authors interview individuals. In other cases, attributions are given with permission. Attributions listed as *Lobby School participant* are from classroom discussions, but I don't recall which participant said it.

When the frankness that makes this book useful would needlessly harm a source, I unilaterally withheld attribution. For example, a lawmaker's words to me in private useful to you should not result in him or her losing campaign contributions or ending up with lower rankings in voter guides.

DISCLAIMER

None of the contributors or organizations with which they are linked necessarily agrees with, endorses, or otherwise has chosen to be associated with anything I have written or with my observations, revelations, or conclusions. I alone am responsible for the content herein.

CHAPTER 1

OVERVIEW OF LOBBYING

LOBBYING DEFINED

Lobbying may be defined as, "trying to influence or gain goodwill." One seeks to influence and gain goodwill in order to sell. This book is about selling legislative products, that is, reasons to support or oppose bills. *Lobbying is legislative sales.*

REASONS TO LOBBY

Lobbying is driven mostly by self-interest. James Madison considered economic self-interest to be the most powerful political motivator. His views may be summarized as *self-interest is the engine of government*, a theme which runs throughout this book. Groups advancing self-interests in Madison's day were called *factions*; today we call them *special-interest groups* or simply *special interests*. Special interests try to achieve nine goals:

1-4. Gain better laws, protect favorable laws, repeal unfavorable laws, and stop adverse bills;

5. Instruct the Governor and courts as to the state's public policy;

6. Affect state executive agencies' rulemaking and enforcement;

7. Build lawmaking momentum among states;

8. Build lawmaking momentum to affect Congress; and

9. Fill holes in Federal law.

Gain better laws, protect favorable laws, repeal unfavorable laws, and stop adverse bills. Using general bills and the proposed state budget, the legislature creates laws regulating individuals and businesses. For all practical purposes, the legislature can do anything it wants to do, good or ill.

Instruct the Governor and courts as to the state's public policy. The state constitution authorizes the legislature by means of statute to assign to the executive, that is, the Governor, and judicial branches broad guiding principles of statutory interpretation and application.

Affect executive agencies' rulemaking and enforcement. Executive agencies are constitutionally required to *implement faithfully* laws enacted by the legislature. The legislature directs them by enacting or repealing their authority and by budget appropriations. However, in practice, legislative authority over agencies may be much less significant than the constitution suggests.

Build lawmaking momentum among states. States fall into genres of interest such that when one state in the genre enacts a particular law, sister states follow creating momentum for other states to adopt similar laws.

Build lawmaking momentum to affect Congress. States' legislation motivates their states' federal delegations to support similar lawmaking in Congress.

Fill holes in Federal law. States plug "holes" in federal regulations. For example, federal regulations may not affect activities below a certain size, dollar amount, number of employees, and the like, thereby leaving the states free to regulate these activities—in effect, to plug the holes in the regulatory framework.

WHO MAY LOBBY

"Everybody" is the answer. The First Amendment to the United States Constitution states, "Congress shall make no law ... abridging the right of the people to ... petition the government for a redress of grievances." This means the U.S. system of government is designed to allow the people to lobby. The result is a *procedurally* transparent system.

The legislative branch is so accessible that W. Allen Moore said, "Do not hire a professional lobbyist unless all else fails. A great deal of money is wasted on lobbyists to open doors that are already open. Senators and their staffs like to help the 'little guy' with a good cause."[1] While legislatures are open to everyone, lawmakers' supporters, voters, and constituents are especially welcome.

However, in exchange for government benefits—especially tax benefits—organizations may choose to accept limitations on their right to lobby, or they may voluntarily surrender advocacy opportunities altogether. States also may limit certain individuals from lobbying including recently retired legislators, certain felons, and persons banned from the legislature for bad conduct.

WHEN TO REGISTER AS A LOBBYIST

An attempt to influence government directly or indirectly, orally or in writing, may be statutorily defined as lobbying. However, an advocate does not need to *register as a lobbyist* until reaching the statutory threshold. Money is the most common, but not the only, trigger. When a client spends money, including hiring a contract lobbyist, there is a good chance it must register.

Do not *presume* because a lobbyist is registered, the client doesn't need to register. We discuss this in Chapter 6, *Ethics Laws for Lobbyists and Clients,* section "Ethics: Client to Lawmaker."

WHOM TO LOBBY

Lobby persons and organizations who can influence a specific bill. In order of relative *political* importance, persons and organizations affecting legislation include:

1. Special interests;

2. Legislative staff;

3. Executive agencies;

4. Legislators;

5. Governor;

6. Lawmakers' supporters;

7. Lawmakers' voters; and

8. Constituents (i.e., general public living in electoral districts).

Seventy percent of winning in the legislature takes place before talking to the first lawmaker. This includes working with 1 through 3. The remaining 30 percent of winning takes place after the legislature receives the bill. Expect 1 through 4 must be lobbied; and perhaps 5. Lobbying 6 through 8 greatly increases chances of success; but the dynamics surrounding a bill may make working with 6 through 8 unnecessary. All this is explained as we work through the book.

Special interests. Special interests direct most legislative activity. They write most bills, build coalitions, line up sponsors and co-sponsors, secure and keep favorable votes, mobilize constituents, gain executive agency support (or at least lack of agency opposition), and build the political momentum to enact statutes.

Legislative staff. The legislature's staff is the second most important group to lobby because these individuals advise legislators on whom to support and how to vote. Legislators normally vote as suggested by staff.

Executive agencies. Agencies are the third most important group to lobby because for all practical purposes they are the legislature's *technical* advisors, and legislators seldom vote contrary to agency advice. Agency support, or at least lack of opposition, is indispensable for most bills.

Legislators. Although first in *constitutional* importance, lawmakers *politically* are quaternary when deciding the fate of a bill. This is because when special interests, legislative staff, and agencies support it, and if it benefits a legislator, he or she will likely vote for the bill.

Governor. The Governor's office is fifth in legislative political importance. But at the same time he or she is first in deciding whether an enrolled[2] bill will become law, and if it does become law how it will be implemented. Whether the Governor's office needs to be lobbied depends on: 1) the Governor's influence with the legislature; 2) the Governor's influence with executive agencies; and 3) the likelihood of a veto.

Lawmakers' supporters. They are legislators' friends, neighbors, fellow church and service members, trusted confidantes, and significant in-state donors whether in or out of lawmakers' districts. They are the best people to carry a message to a lawmaker. To illustrate, I had a bill stuck in a Senate committee when the calendar expired. (The term "calendar" here refers to time-based milestones that bills must pass to continue toward enactment.) The calendar having expired meant the bill was dead for the session. However, our contract lobbyist knew a close friend of the Senate president. He persuaded this close friend to tell the Senate president how good our bill was for the state. The president agreed and obtained unanimous Senate consent to extend the calendar for 30 minutes, thereby springing the bill from committee, to the floor, to the Governor's desk, and into law.

Lawmakers' voters. An election campaign manager says, "Candidates worry about voters. Nobody gives a [expletive deleted] about constituents. Seriously, if you don't vote, then you don't count."[3] After supporters, nothing motivates legislators more than the voters who put and keep them in office.

Constituents (i.e., general public living in the district). Persons whose only connection to the lawmaker is they just happen to reside in the same legislative district as the lawmaker may loosely be called "constituents." Constituents as defined here have small significance in lobbying. *Note: For sake of verbal economy, I will use the term "constituent" as a collective noun to include supporters, voters, and the general public, distinguishing among them as necessary.*

MEDIA

Traditional or Mainstream Media (MSM). The MSM may become involved in a legislative effort. However, expect few *majority party* legislators, advocates, or anyone else trying *to move a bill into law* wants or benefits from media involvement. However, when trying *to kill a bill* both the *minority party* and special interests sharing the politics of reporters may find kindred media spirits ready to help.

Whether liberal or conservative, advocates must be prepared to work with the MSM. A public relations (PR) consultant advises advocates to plan to deal with reporters,

> It's now nearly expected that lobbyists/their clients drum up public concurrence for the higher profile issues or keep them from becoming high profile. Also, PR proactively keeps the opponents from framing the issue into a negative consequence during session and the next election cycle…legislators don't act unless the issue is in the media and special interests don't initiate PR until legislators take action. So which comes first the chicken or the egg? My point is, there is a greater risk in trying to keep it quiet, hoping no one will shine a light. It's better to at least have PR at the strategic table primed and monitoring (which can be inexpensive), but prepared to pull triggers engaging stakeholders…A growing number of issues need to motivate legislators beyond a PAC check and what staff recommends…PR/grassroots lobbying puts faces on complex too-factual/logical issues. Emotion fuels political and PR arguments the lobbying strategy in D.C., and the 50 state capitols.[4]

Social Media. Lobbyists fall into two broad categories of social media users. The first category uses social media to bully lawmakers by fomenting and channeling pressure. The second category uses social media to reward and affirm lawmakers.

Bullying can damage the goodwill on which long-term influence and lawmaker cooperation and support are founded. This is not to say this approach isn't at times effective but to say it's not sustainable for long-term effective lobbying.

The second category of lobbyists attempts to persuade by building positive relationships. A lobbyist writes,

We mainly use social media to thank our legislators for their support, giving them a shout out to the people who support the same issues, but we don't see them as lobbying tools. On a federal level, for us, Twitter has been a good resource for thanking legislators for their support of bills. On a state level, there are very few legislators that use Twitter enough to be on the same level as federal. It's more utilized for educating the general public on why we would support an issue, and one way to help shape the general consensus on a topic.[5]

Legislators realizing social media are avatars, fake Facebook pages, banks of trolls, bots, and click farms, should ignore much of it. And it can backfire. The president of a health care network cautions, "Personally, I am uncomfortable with using social media as a lobbying tool representing my company's interests as I am not sure how I would control the message. I worry statements could get misinterpreted, go viral and the resulting damage may outstrip the benefits."[6]

WHEN TO LOBBY

Lobbying needs to start well before the beginning of the legislative session. In *most* but not all jurisdictions, lobbying a bill into law is more difficult and takes much more work than stopping a bill from becoming law. If the process of securing lawmakers' support hasn't begun well before the session starts, avoidable and unnecessary difficulty is added to achieving legislative goals. To kill a bill, however, one well-placed lobbyist with political "chits"[7] with one key legislator or the Governor can *defeat* legislation. If a client or lobbyist doesn't have chits, then the time to begin depends on the political momentum behind the bill.

WHERE TO LOBBY

Lobbying is done in the capitol building, in lawmakers' districts, and in the capital city where special interests and their lobbyists reside.

In the capitol amid the frenzy, distractions, and political cross-winds of the legislative session, advocates build on legislators' initial support or interest developed from pre-session visits. *For the rest of this book, I use the term "capital" as a collective noun that includes the capitol, that is, the building in which lawmakers officially meet to do the people's business and the city in which the capitol building is found.*

Trust Is the Foundation of Effective Lobbying

Trust is the foundation of immediate and long-term influence. Advocates' *integrity* is indispensable. When legislators trust them, they listen to them; and if they don't trust them, lawmakers won't hear a word they say. Lawmakers take advocates seriously when they believe advocates abide by the three elements of trust: scrupulous honesty, accuracy, and credibility.

> **Scrupulous honesty.** Scrupulous honesty means clients and lobbyists are transparent and forthright with government officials, avoiding half-truths or otherwise spinning stories to withhold information unfavorable to clients. To maintain legislators' trust, advocates must update them as circumstances rewrite their narratives. They are in front of their story; meaning being the first ones to disclose positive and negative developments that could influence legislators' positions on bills. Arkansas State Senator Uvalde Lindsey says he does not trust lobbyists who are, "technically accurate but not totally forthright."[8]

One lie to a legislator can ruin a lobbyist's career. To illustrate, a large group of corporate lobbyists was meeting with several members of the Florida legislature at a posh resort. The chairman of the committee with which we were most concerned named a D.C. lobbyist whom we all knew saying, "[Name of lobbyist] lied to us once, he'll lie to us again, and he'd better never show his face again before the Florida Senate Natural Resources

Committee."[9] This lobbyist's career with the Florida legislature was interrupted for several years until everyone to whom he lied was term-limited out of office.

Accuracy. Accuracy means providing reasonable and reproducible estimates of the expected effects of a bill. For example, if an advocate says a law will cost the government 11 million dollars, it had better cost between 10.5 and 11.5 million dollars. Opponents and the legislature's budget office also tell lawmakers their estimates, which are checks on advocates. Legislators know estimates fall within ranges, so as long as they are somewhat near the correct number, outcome, or result, advocates will be credible. However, legislatures distrust advocates whose estimates seem unrealistic.

Credibility. Credibility means abiding by three sets of rules: written; unwritten; unwritten and unspoken. Written rules are found on the legislature's website and include the constitution, statutes, joint rules of the legislature, rules of each of the two chambers, rules peculiar to a particular committee or subcommittee, and the rules of any of the legislative service offices. Of the entire body of rules, only a small portion applies to lobbying.

Lobbying, like all professions, has an unwritten but expected code of conduct. Sometimes an unwritten code is called *etiquette*. For example, lobbying etiquette demands advocates speak to all parties with a legitimate interest in their bill *whether they want to or not*. More bluntly, the rule is, "You have to talk to people you don't like and who don't like you."

Finally, there is the unwritten and unspoken rule which can be expressed, "You help me and I help you. And if I help you and then you don't help me, don't bother coming back again." Lobbying is fueled by the exchange of favors, albeit the exchange is never verbalized. It's not *quid pro quo*, but it's not far from it.

AGENCIES REQUIRE TRUST, TOO

Executive agencies expect scrupulous honesty and accuracy from advocates. While technically competent, they do not have adequate resources to check every assertion, especially in regard to the effects of proposed legislation. They assume advocates know their businesses and operations better than agencies do. A good word about a bill from the agency skyrockets its chances of legislative success; a bad word can kill it.

LEGISLATIVE PROCEDURE AND LOBBYING
ARE SIMILAR IN ALL STATES

One lobbyist can work in many different jurisdictions because the techniques of advocacy are pretty much the same, regardless of jurisdiction. This situation occurs for three reasons:

1.   The U.S. Constitution sets procedures for federal and state governments;

2.   Legislators are remarkably similar to one another in personality type and ambition; and

3.   Making a "sale" is the ultimate goal.

The U.S. Constitution sets procedures for federal and state governments. The U.S. Constitution's Fifth and Fourteenth Amendments' "Due Process" and "Equal Treatment" clauses impose citizen-protective requirements on government action so that, despite small differences such as sequence of steps, the 99 state legislative chambers process bills similarly.[10]

For an idea to become law, it must be presented to the legislature in the constitutionally prescribed form called a *bill*. "No law shall be enacted

11

except by bill" is common constitutional language. Although states vary as to details, the process generally goes as follows:

The first stage involves drafting and sponsoring the bill. A bill is conceived by a special interest, a lawmaker, Governor's office, or executive agency. The vast majority of bills are proposed by special interests.

Each bill must have a sponsor. In most states, a sponsor is a legislator or legislative committee. In some states, executive agencies or the Governor may sponsor a bill. The sponsor submits the idea for or draft of a bill to the chamber's office of bill drafting services which ensures the bill-draft is in proper form and reflects the sponsor's intentions. It assigns a number to the bill-draft and returns it to the sponsor; the group for whom the legislator is sponsoring the bill may try to add additional sponsors.

The second stage involves moving the bill-draft forward. The sponsor sends the bill-draft to administrative staff of his or her chamber, called the *chamber of origin,* who assigns the bill an identifying number, either the original bill-draft number or a new one. For the rest of the session, the bill's status can be monitored via that number.

The chamber of origin considers or *reads* the bill three times. On *first reading* (sometimes before) chamber management—political or administrative—sends or *refers* the bill to appropriate committees, called *committees of referral,* for review, discussion, revision, and *recommendation.* Populated by several lawmakers and assisted by professional staffs, committees do the detailed work on the bill. Committee recommendations to the chamber, called *reports,* suggest to the chamber actions the committee thinks the chamber should take regarding the bill.

The first committee to consider the bill is the *committee of first referral* which generally is the committee of *subject matter jurisdiction*. That is, health care bills are referred to the health committee, environmental bills to the environmental committee, agricultural bills to the agricultural committee, and so on. The fewer committees of referral the better. A bill sent to several committees of referral may find that time expires before all of the committees can process it; and many referrals give opponents many opportunities to amend it unfavorably. A bill proposing to spend state money goes to one or more fiscal committees, called *Ways and Means, Finance, Budget*, or something similar, for approval.

Any committee of referral may recommend to the chamber changes to the bill, called *amendments*. Each proposed amendment is reviewed by the chamber's legal services before being considered by the full chamber.

A bill favorably reported *as amended* (or not amended) by all committees of jurisdiction is sent to the chamber for action. If any committee does not report a bill or unfavorably reports it to the chamber floor, the bill is likely dead.

The third stage deals with chamber action. On *second reading* the chamber considers and debates the committee's report. On *third reading* the chamber approves or disapproves the bill. Scheduling of readings is done by chamber leadership or administration, or by a committee which may be called the *Rules Committee* or *Calendar Committee*, and this committee also may decide the rules for debate. A bill may get through every committee of referral and then die for lack of action in the Rules Committee.

If the chamber approves the bill it is *engrossed* showing the bill after all the changes. The chamber of origin then sends—that is, *messages*—the engrossed bill to the *receiving* or *second chamber*. The receiving chamber follows a procedure similar to the above. If that chamber approves the bill unchanged, the bill goes back to the chamber of origin for final action.

Each chamber must pass the identical bill. If the second chamber amends the bill such that the two chambers' versions of the bill are not identical, the bill may be sent to a *conference committee* made up of members from both chambers, so that a compromise can be reached. However, conference committees require considerable effort on behalf of the chambers so in many states unless a bill is really important to leadership, don't expect it to go conference. Disagreement between the chambers means the bill is dead.

If the bill passes both chambers, it is certified, that is, *enrolled*, by the leaders of each chamber as an *enactment*. The enactment is sent to the Governor.

The final stages involve the Governor, Secretary of State, and executive agencies. The Governor may sign the enactment, allow it to become law without the Governor's signature, or veto it. If the Governor allows it to become law, it is now an *act*. If the Governor *vetoes* the enactment, it is dead unless the legislature *overrides* the Governor's objections. An override requires a constitutionally defined majority vote in each chamber. Chapter 12, *Lobbying the Governor*, section "Vetoes," discusses this more. If the veto is overridden the enactment becomes an act.

The Secretary of State codifies portions of the act that have wide application. Codified portions are called *statutes* and are entered into the law books. Laws of limited application, such as the budget, resolves, and local laws—for example, naming a bridge—are compiled into a separate volume called the *laws of the state*. At last, the statute is passed to the executive agency responsible for drawing up *rules* for implementing and enforcing the new law.

Legislators are remarkably similar to one another in personality type and ambition. Individual and collective personalities, rather than structural differences, influence how one state legislature differs from another, how one legislative chamber or committee differs from another in the same state, and why one motivator works better with one lawmaker and not with another.

"Making a sale" is the ultimate goal. Using the metaphor *making a sale* provides insight into and guidance for lobbying. Like everyone else in the lobbying process, legislators are driven by self-interest. Legislators and lobbyists are legally selling something the other wants. Legislators have votes which are what special interests want. Special interests offer help to lawmakers in achieving lawmakers' ambitions. This exchange is called *politics*.

LOBBYING IS MOSTLY ABOUT MONEY

James Madison observed people use government to enrich themselves. He said, "Every shilling with which they overburden the inferior number, is a shilling saved to their own pockets."[11] Then as now, at least in my personal observation, 85 percent of lobbying is about taking money from one person's pocket and putting it into someone else's pocket.

Profit making groups lobby the legislature to favor one business, product, or industry over another, or to favor business over labor. Labor unions lobby to enrich themselves and their members, and to get advantages over management, businesses, and the government. Charities lobby to gain government appropriations to carry out their missions and pay their employees. Professions lobby to protect their members' interests, to limit marketplace competition from other professions and from unlicensed providers, and for public welfare. Local governments lobby to obtain appropriations, and local legislative and taxing authority. "Public interest" groups lobby to protect the public, but their work usually enriches themselves by getting budget appropriations, grants from an agency, or fundraising donations.

FOLLOW THE MONEY

Given most lobbying is about transferring money from one interest group to another, the first rule for understanding which groups might be interested in an advocacy effort is this, *follow the money*. By following the money, clients can estimate who may support or oppose them and their degrees of involvement. To follow the money, consider the following:

Who pays the bill? Will it be state or local government? Will it be funded by an agency's operating budget, by the general state fund, by an increase in taxes, or by private money? Of course a few or many taxpayers have to pay the bill because for government to benefit one interest, it has to burden, that is, take money away from, another interest.

Where will the money go? Government spends money on public goals and projects and it mandates how private persons spend their money.

Who wants the money? All those who stand to gain or lose money will be vitally interested in the bill and will lobby the legislature to obtain more money, take someone's money, or keep someone else from taking theirs.

How much money is involved? The amount of money at stake determines how much groups invest in terms of their lobbying dollars, political capital, and other elements of influence. The more money involved in the transfer, the larger the number of parties involved in the process, and the greater the intensity of their lobbying.

Fiscal notes as predictive tools. State legislatures estimate the financial impact of legislation on state and local governments. These estimates, which are developed for each appropriation financially affecting state or local government, are called *fiscal notes* and accompany a bill throughout the legislative process. Although fiscal notes won't necessarily consider state-mandated transfers of private funds to private parties, these notes can nevertheless be valuable in predicting special interests that may become involved in lobbying for or against draft legislation.

WHEN LOBBYING IS LESS ABOUT MONEY

Primary advocates. Some who initiate lawmaking, whom I call *primary advocates*, are not driven *exclusively* by their own financial advantages. They generally are nonprofit or not-for-profit and lobby to make the world a better place (at least in their view). They want money for social causes, such as serving the homeless; philosophical goals, such as promoting energy independence; ideological causes, such as "more government is needed" or "less government is needed"; political goals, such as making their organization look better to the lawmakers who fund them; or strategic goals, such as promoting weak legislation to head off future onerous legislation. Providing services costs money, and many primary advocates can pay their bills only when funded by government. Yes, they want state money but as a means to achieve social goods.

Secondary Advocates. *Secondary advocates* seek financial advantage by helping primary advocates achieve their goals. That is, those lobbying for a social good may join forces with those lobbying to advance their business interests. Thus, when I advised primary advocates for *Home and Community-Based Services* for Medicaid patients, the net result was an estimated annual transfer of $500 million per year of state money from nursing homes to alternative care providers. Both the primary advocates and the secondary advocates profited in their own ways.

SUMMARY CHAPTER 1

To influence the enactment of a bill, in order of importance, advocates lobby special interests, legislative staff, executive agency staff, legislators, perhaps the Governor's office, lawmakers' supporters and voters, constituents, and the media. Generally, when special interests, legislative staff, and executive agencies agree, and a proposal has some advantage for a legislator, he or she will vote for it. The chances of a lawmaker voting for a bill are further increased when his or her supporters and voters like the bill.

The U.S. system of lawmaking, by law and by expectation, demands advocates are scrupulously honest, accurate, and credible. Most lobbying is about taking money from one person's pocket and putting it into someone else's pocket. By following the money, advocates can estimate their legislative friends and enemies and start working with them to maximize consensus and reduce conflict.

The rest of lobbying is driven by primary advocates hoping to advance what they see as benefits to society. Secondary advocates profit by selling products, services, or both to primary advocates and those they serve.

We have overviewed the what, how, who, why, when, and where of lobbying and emphasized advocates must be trustworthy and honorable. In Chapter 2, *Understanding Contract Lobbyists*, we explain who lobbyists are, how they think, and what they do for their clients.

UNDERSTANDING CONTRACT LOBBYISTS

Lobbyists are so influential that for almost 150 years they have been called the *Third House* of the legislature. They can help a client greatly, or be wholly unnecessary.

WHAT LOBBYISTS DO FOR CLIENTS

Lobbyists do for clients what clients cannot do for themselves or they help clients lobby better; in either case they improve clients' probabilities of legislative success. They guide clients through the legislature's procedural nuances and the advocacy process. This includes how to effectively interact with legislators, legislative staff, agency staff, special interests, and the Governor. A client absent from the capital needs a lobbyist. A contract lobbyist can make a politically powerful client more successful.

On the other hand, a lobbyist may be an unnecessary expense, and the wrong one could be a client's undoing. Former lobbyist and U.S. Senator Marlow Cook said, "Many people in Washington, D.C., who are paid big money produce little. Some lobbyists encourage their clients to get into projects the clients could effectively lobby themselves or lobby issues that are dead in the water from the outset, or take money for allegedly lobbying a project that is no problem from the beginning, or purposely drag out an issue to make more money."[12]

WHAT LOBBYISTS OFFER

Contract lobbyists offer clients:

Objectivity. This quality permits the lobbyist to tell the client the truth even if it means dashing its hopes or losing the client. Independence is the foundation of objectivity. A lobbyist can be objective when a client's success or failure with the legislature *does not* affect the lobbyist's long-term well-being. A client should find a new lobbyist if for emotional or financial reasons the lobbyist needs the client.

Good name. A well-respected lobbyist lends to the client his or her personal credibility, which is especially useful for a client unknown in the capital. Conversely, association with a lobbyist who is not respected could prove harmful, so an accurate appraisal of the lobbyist's reputation is important.

Principal list. Clients, that is, principals and their employee-representatives, if any, make the lobbyist. A lobbyist's degree of influence with legislators and other special interests is proportional to the collective *gravitas* of the lobbyist's clients.

Relationships. In all sales including lobbying, relationships are central. Lobbyists use their associations to introduce clients to those impacting clients' bills, advise clients on how to deal with them, and avoid those who are irrelevant or detrimental to moving a bill.

Credits and liabilities. A lobbyist has from zero to several political credits with lawmakers that is, "chits"[13], he or she might "cash in." A lobbyist also may have liabilities reducing his or her utility to a client.

Process expertise. Lawmaking is complex procedurally and politically, and sometimes process expertise is necessary to navigate both the logical and the seemingly irrational aspects of lawmaking. A lobbyist understanding the intricacies of formal and informal legislative procedure may be able to shepherd a bill past seemingly insurmountable obstacles.

Advice on ethics compliance. Lobbyists advise clients about compliance with ethics laws. Ethics noncompliance can be disastrous to an advocacy campaign.

Coalition building. A lobbyist's personal knowledge of special interests and his or her experience in creating, leading, and serving on coalitions is a tremendous asset to a lobbying campaign. Few substantive bills move without the support of coalitions.

Consensus building. In lobbying, consensus propels and controversy kills. A lobbyist must be skilled in building consensus. Former U.S. Sen. Mark Hatfield said, "People expect the lobbyist to be an advocate, but his basic task is to reconcile diverse viewpoints, to develop a consensus through compromise and accommodation; that is the essence of lobbying. He is a mediator, a reconciler, and an arbiter as well as an advocate."[14]

Grassroots development. Lobbyists organize and apply grassroots power. Supporters, voters, and constituents trump lobbyists as explained below. James Leahy, Esq., a well-established Connecticut lobbyist commented, "Today most legislative campaigns are won and lost on the strength of the grassroots."[15]

Coaching. Lobbyists show clients how to navigate the capital and use their political strength most effectively. They also coach clients on accruing chits especially when developing their own in-house government affairs programs.

Intelligence, strategy, and tactics. Political intelligence means the latest gossip not found in the "Today in the Legislature" newsletter.

Strategy is the overall plan of action and statement of major goals. Tactics involve applying the right resources to the right person at the right moment.

Realism. Lobbyists assist clients in formulating goals having the greatest potential of winning in the legislative session or may counsel the client that this is not the right time to go to the legislature.

Capital presence. Active presence in the capital is a key service supplied by a lobbyist. Being physically present in the capital, lobbyists constantly interact with lawmakers, staffs, agencies, and special interests. Attune to the undercurrents in the capital, they can jump to the client's defense when unanticipated threats suddenly appear, or seize unexpected positive opportunities. When the client is not in the capital, the lobbyist serves as the client's surrogate—at least in noncritical matters.

"Herding cats." A lobbyist ensures that everyone associated with the lobbying campaign is doing what they need to be doing when it needs to be done. He or she should be a good coach coordinating the efforts of each player on the team.

Confidante status. The few lobbyists achieving the status of "legislative confidante" are valued by legislators as trusted sources of information, conduits of communication between warring legislators and between legislators and interest groups, bearers of "breaking news" or political intelligence, and safe "sounding boards" to legislators. To illustrate, a lobbyist was summoned by the Speaker of the House to intervene with a House member whose sexual philandering with female lobbyists was becoming an embarrassment to the House and the party. This particular lobbyist was asked to help because of his long relationship with the lawmaker's father and the member.

Return on investment (ROI). The ROI for those employing lobbyists can be profound. Alex Blumberg referred to work by Raquel Alexander and Susan Scholz comparing taxes saved by lobbying entities with the amount the firms spent lobbying for a specific tax law: "Their research showed the return on lobbying for those multinational corporations was 22,000 percent. That means for every dollar spent on lobbying, the companies got $220 in tax benefits."[16]

WHAT LOBBYISTS DO NOT OFFER

On the other hand lobbyists don't offer:

Personal political power. In most cases, the lobbyist's *personal political power*—his or her individual ability to move a bill into law without strong client participation—is more image than reality. Donald deKieffer, speaking about lobbying in Washington, D.C., said, "[F]ew if any professional lobbyists have a significant degree of personal political power."[17] In my view, this also applies at the state level, with one qualifier: The larger the state, the more it is true and the smaller the state, perhaps the less it is true.

Face to the media. A client shouldn't expect its lobbyist to be its face to the media. Most lobbyists avoid drawing attention to themselves, their clients, bills on which they are working, deals they are making, and friendly legislators and special interests critical to moving a bill into law. A Washington, D.C. (henceforth just "D.C.") lobbyist advises, "A good lobbyist is like a CIA agent. If we've done our job, nobody knows our name."[18] Lawmakers, not lobbyists, should be in the public eye.

Replacing the client. A contract lobbyist cannot do for the client what the client should be doing for itself. James Leahy remarks, "Your lobbyist can keep you in the game, but you have to put yourself across the goal line ... Lobbyists are good for strategy development and contacts, but association members must provide the energy and issue expertise."[19] Lobbyists cannot and should not make decisions belonging to the client.

An automatic belief in the client's cause. A lobbyist is a consultant, a mercenary of sorts, which is why lobbyists sometimes are referred to as "hired guns." A client should no more expect its lobbyist to become a true believer in its particular cause than he or she should become a true believer in any of the causes of his or her other clients. This is especially true for a firm having many clients. Former Congressman Ed Jenkins observed as to D.C. lobbyists, "A lobbyist is a hired gun and can take either side of an issue, like a lawyer."[20] Becoming a true believer may happen, but clients can't expect or demand it. Lobbyists, like lawyers, are employed to represent their clients competently and to the best of their abilities. They do so to the degree that representing a client advances their own business interests.

THE HOME-FOLK TRUMP ALL LOBBYISTS

Supporters, voters, and constituents are major influencers upon lawmakers, as is emphasized throughout this book. Former Congressman Mark Foley advises,

> I always believed that the most effective lobbying while I was in elective office was when a local advocate from my district accompanied the paid lobbyist to bring a personal perspective to the issue at hand. Whether it was advocating for insurance reform or diabetes research the words from a local voter kept in the forefront of my mind that it wasn't an exercise in pleasing the hired gun but reinforcing my ties to my local community.[21]

This means in *moving a bill*, if the contest is between a major-leaguer versus a minor-leaguer, and there is *no home-folk involvement*, then bet on the major-leaguer. If the contest is between a major-leaguer with no support from the district versus a minor-leaguer *with home-folk involvement,* then bet on the minor-leaguer. If the contest is between a major-leaguer and a minor-leaguer, and *both or neither have home-folk involvement,* then a lawmaker's support can go either way. Below I discuss spectator, minor-league, and major-league lobbyists.

However, in *killing a bill,* bet on the major-leaguer willing to spend political chits. This is because the insider-relationship, deal-making, *friends-helping-friends* exchanges of favors are at play, and the bill extermination process takes place behind the scenes and out of sight. Major-leaguers trade on these relationships that produce results for their clients. To illustrate, a *Lobby School* participant for a household name corporation told me he had hired a lobbyist to move a bill. As his bill was gaining traction, he learned his opponents had hired as their lobbyist a "drinking buddy" of the chairman of the committee through which the bill had to pass. Upon hearing of this hire, his company dropped its legislative effort. I told him he made the right decision because all it takes is one lobbyist to cash in one chit with one well-placed lawmaker such as a committee chair.

On the other hand, I had a lawmaker, *after promising me* a vote two hours earlier, reverse herself because her home-folk—supporters, voters, and constituents—rose up against my bill. Other lobbyists have told me similar stories. No lobbyist beats the home-folk when it comes to getting lawmakers' votes. As former Tennessee Speaker of the Senate Ron Ramsey once said, "In politics the voter is always right."[22]

CULTURE TRUMPS STRATEGY

Related to the "Home-Folk Trump All Lobbyists" is, *culture trumps strategy.* Strategy, the art and science of planning and marshalling resources for their most efficient and effective use, is important.

However, the culture in which strategy functions is more influential as to motivating lawmakers to vote a client's way. In lobbying, the culture is that of a lawmaker's supporters, voters, and to a lesser degree, constituents. Business coach Nilofer Merchant comments, "The best strategic idea means nothing in isolation. If the strategy conflicts with how a group of people already believes, behaves or makes decisions, then it fails. Conversely, a culturally robust team can turn a so-so strategy into a winner."[23]

A client cannot ignore culture. *Regionalism is reality.* To illustrate, *Lobby School* participants from the Northeast often have difficulty understanding the importance of religion to Southern lawmakers. For example, while 19 percent of Maine lawmakers self-identify as Christian, those numbers in Tennessee are 99 percent, Mississippi 96 percent, Alabama 93 percent, Florida 88 percent, and so forth. A lobbyist's shocked expression upon hearing a lawmaker's staff say, "Have a blessed day" creates a small but unnecessary negative bias.

A client employing a culturally sensitive strategy, having the support of the lawmaker's home-folk, and having the assets described above, may not need a contract lobbyist at all. Or it may use an unlobbyist or registered lobbyist, not to lobby, but to advise how to use its political strength. We begin by discussing the "unlobbyist."

UNREGISTERED GOVERNMENT AFFAIRS COUNSELORS: "UNLOBBYISTS"

In recent years, unregistered, limited-service, government affairs counselors have become more common. The *New York Times* dubbed them the *unlobbyists.* Unlobbyists' names are not found on the state's lobbyist roster. Their clients are undisclosed, and their fees are unknown.

These expert counselors advise clients on the best use of clients' political resources. They do not lobby as "lobbying" is defined by state ethics law; rather they help their clients lobby better.

Unlobbyists have certain drawbacks. First, their services are limited by law, compared to those of a registered lobbyist. Second, registered lobbyists, lawmakers, and staffs may consider unlobbyists to be acting outside the law and therefore resist working with their clients. Third, should an unregistered counselor be caught encroaching on state regulated advocacy, an ethics accusation could taint a client even if it is only "guilt by association." On the other hand, for organizations not looking for representation but for behind-the-scenes advice, unlobbyists may be attractive.

A client should register as a lobbyist when using an unlobbyist. Otherwise, a client found to be lobbying while unregistered could be subject to prosecution and public embarrassment.

DO NOT USE AN UNREGISTERED LOBBYIST

Using persons not registered as lobbyists but who are required to register per state law can lead to significant legal and political problems for the client, its lobbyist, and its bill. State lobbyist registration offices are on the lookout for unregistered lobbyists. For example, the Rhode Island Department of State has this admonition on its website, "If you have reason to believe that an individual or entity currently not registered in our Lobby Tracker system is engaged in the practice of lobbying a Rhode Island state official please use the form below to send us a detailed and anonymous tip. Thank you."[24]

To avoid registering as lobbyists, some organizations refuse to admit they are lobbying. Instead of *lobbying*, they describe their behavior as *advocating, educating, providing information, communicating with our elected representatives*, and so on. However, statutes define what behavior is and isn't lobbying. Failure to conform to ethics laws may lead to administrative, civil, or criminal prosecution resulting in fines or jail time, loss of public image, perhaps loss of tax-exempt status for 501(c)(3) IRC organizations, and in all cases loss of credibility with the legislature and special interests.

A client having sufficient political power, including the ability to mobilize lawmakers' supporters, may find an unlobbyist useful. On the other hand, for a client having insufficient political power or wanting to improve its chances of winning, a registered contract lobbyist is the way to go.

REGISTERED LOBBYISTS

Registered lobbyists can be grouped as spectators, minor-leaguers, or major-leaguers.[25] Three key elements determine into which category a lobbyist fits: clients, strength of lobbyist's personality, and relationships, both the lobbyist's relationships and those of his or her clients. Depending upon particular circumstances, any of the three kinds of lobbyists may meet a client's needs. I touch upon spectators and minor-leaguers and then focus upon major-leaguers who are *capital players*.

SPECTATOR AND MINOR-LEAGUE LOBBYISTS

Spectators and their clients either don't desire to or can't influence the legislature. Spectators may join a coalition to put their names on its membership roster, monitor committee meetings, or attend fundraisers. At most, spectators supply additional facts and analyses beyond those provided by subscription capitol news services.

Minor-leaguers serve principals having modest resources; or principals having considerable resources but for whom the costs and conflicts associated with hiring a capital player are overkill relative to the task at hand. In larger states, minor-leaguers are more likely to be found providing technical assistance to legislative staff rather than politicking with legislators. They don't politick as much because they don't have the client base that gets them in with key lawmakers. Therefore, while many minor-league lobbyists have major-league personalities, they remain in the minors but once they secure that first big name client, they move up into the major-league.

CLIENTS MAKE THE LOBBYIST

Clients profoundly affect a contract lobbyist's level of personal power, influence, marketability, and income. A North Carolina legislator said of a particular lobbyist, "He represents those who have power, so he has power. Anybody with his list of clients, and the resources and clout they bring with them, would do well in the General Assembly."[26]

Major-leaguers are not necessarily more competent as lobbyists than minor-leaguers. There is no reason to presume inferior service from a minor-leaguer or superior service from a major-leaguer. Minor-leaguers can do almost anything a major-leaguer can do except *personally* influence lawmakers, again because they don't have big name clients.

Minor-leaguers have difficulty signing substantial clients; and major-leaguers have continuing success because *clients of a feather flock together.* Powerful clients want to be associated with fellow powerful clients because their mutual association increases the political muscle of each. In a sense, they form a coalition around a major-league lobbyist. This is not a typical coalition based on a common legislative goal but a coalition of power formed by being clients of the same high status lobbying firm.

However, getting its first big name can be very difficult for a minor-leaguer because the powerful often do not want to be associated with the less powerful. And "principal stealing," that is, competing for another lobbyist's clients, violates lobbyist etiquette and some states' lobbyist associations' ethics. Big name clients usually go to the major-leaguers; other clients, with some exceptions, go to the minor-leaguers.

ADVANTAGES OF MINOR-LEAGUE LOBBYISTS

A minor-league lobbyist might be perfect for a client's needs. I define "need" as the difference between the political power a client has and the amount of political power required to accomplish its goal. Smaller firms well attune to legislative and agency gossip and procedures may be suitable in terms of both fees and services.

A minor-league firm can be attractive because it can make a client "high priority." The manager of a multistate lobbying program comments,

> There are several considerations when selecting a long-term lobbyist; however, there is one consideration above all else that has helped our company gain influence...While we retain a lobbyist in every state in which we operate, our company is very budget conscious and allocates funds quite lightly for those lobbyists. This has forced us to look past the more established—expensive—firms and turn to those lobbyists who are just setting out on their own and who are willing to cut us a good deal to secure one of their first long-term contracts. By selecting newly minted contractors with in-house corporate experience, we have mitigated the risk of selecting a poor performer with no contacts.
>
> Today, our contractors are well-established independent lobbyists with respectable client rosters and strong connections at the

capitol; however, we still enjoy preferential treatment as their oldest client…and still at a bargain price. In fact, when our company had a policy of making no political contributions, often the only political asset we had was the 'first client' loyalty of a lobbyist who had banked political capital using PAC dollars from their other clients. (We've since changed our practice and are now contributing equally to the campaign process.)

So if a friend of mine were looking for a long-term lobbyist relationship, I would highly recommend that they ignore the well-established capitol gorillas and look for a spunky, in-house corporate lobbyist who is looking for his or her first client to strike-out on his or her own. It's the 'buy low' strategy for legislative advocacy![27]

A client with sufficient political power may meet its lobbying needs using the hard work, dedication, advice, counsel, and direction of a minor-league lobbyist.

MAJOR-LEAGUE FIRMS ARE NOT ALWAYS THE BEST OR MOST COST-EFFECTIVE CHOICE

A client may find a major-leaguer much more than what is necessary for the task at hand and, therefore, not worth the higher fees, inherent (yet manageable) conflicts of interest among prestigious clients, and the chance of being of lesser importance than more famous, better paying, or long-term clients. A client not paying big fees, or not demanding attention from the contract lobbyist, may find itself lost on a roster having several large or too many other clients.

Expect lobbyists to give priority to the demands of big name clients. George A. Dalley while still staff to Congressman Charles Rangel said,

I hesitate to recommend lobbyists to constituents, but if asked I try to give a person options. I tend to recommend the small, lesser known lobbyists. Large lobbying firms have many clients, and I sense that none of them gets the close attention or specialized services that small firms provide...Also try to get a lobbyist who isn't juggling a number of issues and clients, who will place your issue at the top of his agenda and who already has relationships with Members, because you don't want to subsidize his establishment of such relationships.[28]

On the other hand, if the task requires political power lifting and a client doesn't have political horsepower, then a major-league lobbyist may be necessary.

MAJOR-LEAGUE LOBBYISTS AND IMPORTANT PERSONALITY TRAITS

Major-league lobbyists have substantial clients, strong personalities, and key personal relationships. They are the "insiders." Most of them have been in the lobbying business a long time, and they tend to be older. Successful lobbyists have the following traits, but major-league lobbyists have them in greater measure.

High emotional intelligence. Legislative lobbying is a highly irrational process, so "emotional intelligence" (EI) is a great asset. Definitions vary, but generally EI is the ability to perceive emotions in others, understand the relationship among emotions and how emotions influence or feed other emotions, use emotions in thinking and problem solving, and manage emotions to achieve goals.

Skilled client management. A lobbyist has to control clients' expectations to be perceived as an asset, even amidst what seems to be the lobbyist's failure. To do this, he or she must be proficient in responding with messages crafted to anticipate and respond to client concerns. Further, client management means making the client feel like he or she is important; perhaps even more important than the client really is.

Self-assurance. Lobbyists must be able to inspire confidence to sell legislative products to special interests, legislative and agency staffs, legislators, the Governor's office, and others. They convey to clients they know what to do, they know how to do it, and they have resources to meet their client's needs. This state of affairs may or may not be true, but it's what they project.

Subtle or overt arrogance. Some lobbyists use their arrogance to dominate and manipulate others, including their own clients. I have been in enough meetings with major-league lobbyists to see them dismiss minor-league lobbyists and even other major-leaguers.

Ability to work in small spaces. There is little room for lobbyists to make many meaningful decisions in the lawmaking process. Major policy decisions belong to the client. Client and contract lobbyists make up one team advocating for one bill among many or even thousands of other teams and bills competing for the legislature's short and limited attention. With a small issue, the lobbyist may have a small space all to him or herself. With a big issue, the space is small because so many people are occupying it.

Ability to influence on the margins. Forces abound over which lobbyists have little control, and there may be few opportunities to affect the legislative process in major ways. These forces typically include the theme of the legislative session, partisanship of the legislature, interest group dynamics, volatile capitol relationships, other clients' demands, hidden agendas, secret deals, and the vagaries of politics. Within a context that would seem overwhelming in size and complexity, major-league lobbyists often are able to obtain small changes that have big results for their clients.

33

RELATIONSHIP RECIPROCITY

Relationship reciprocity is the emotional connection lawmakers and major-league lobbyists develop leading to the mutual conclusion *we have to take care of each other*. Robert Wechsler advises, "More than anything, it is personal relationships that enable lobbyists and clients to get access to government officials and to get preferential treatment relating to the special benefits they are seeking. Connections are also something that lobbyists brag about to their potential clients, even on their websites."[29]

Craig Holman, Ph.D., Public Citizen, and Thomas Susman, Esq., American Bar Association, write, "In their role of creating a bridge between the private sector and the public sector, lobbyists and public officials instinctively relate according to the 'reciprocity principle,' in which lobbyists providing needed research, gifts or other items of value help create a sense of obligation on behalf of appreciative public officials."[30]

The sense of obligation and the process of working on their relationships can lead to lobbyists securing a greater measure of lawmakers' votes. That's why lobbyists invite lawmakers to fly together on private airplanes, party together at resorts, and share private retreats. Lobbyists cultivate these relationships. Relationship reciprocity may even be built without one, or both, of the parties realizing what's going on.

In my years dealing with the powerful, I have seen the magnetism the powerful have for each other. The magnetism may draw them together, or the magnetism may push them apart. Nevertheless, it's an almost metaphysical force. Upon meeting, each senses it in the other. Major-league lobbyists have cultivated it, often for years, and they skillfully project it. Some lawmakers are attracted to it because it caters to their "I want to be a rock star" mentality and "Acquired Situational Narcissism."

However, as discussed throughout this book, a major-league lobbyist's chits, golf games, private planes, campaign contributions, bar tabs, and even the lawmaker's hopes for a job, are no match for the home-folk. Lawmakers are not going to vote against their own interests as embodied in keeping supporters, voters, and constituents on their side.

PRESSURES ON ALL LOBBYISTS

Pressures common to all lobbyists stem from the need to run a money making business and forces over which they have little control. Some pressures affecting a lobbyist's behavior include:

Operating a profitable business. A contract lobbyist is in business to make money. And like other business people, a lobbyist continually weighs his or her own business interests against those of his or her clients. How can a lobbyist keep clients, find new and better clients, and prevent other lobbyists from taking their clients? How does he or she obtain the money to build and maintain relationships with lawmakers? How does he or she end a relationship with a problematic client? All of these questions must necessarily reside in the back of a lobbyist's mind as he or she balances a variety of factors influencing whether or not the lobbyist will be able to make payroll, pay the rent, and earn a good living.

Without war there is no profitable business. As with all mercenaries without war there is no money. Lobbyists don't make money in peaceful times. Conflict is in their interest and occasionally to generate business they foment it themselves.

Jeffrey H. Birnbaum notes, "In the volatile world of Washington lobbying, victory was sweet but chaos was sweeter. For a lobbyist nothing was better than a long, even bitter, legislative battle and nothing was worse than a final resolution. Constant conflict was what kept coffers brimming. Peace means only poverty."[31] Because resolving a client's legislative problems may not always be in a lobbyist's financial best interests, a lobbyist may face a business pressure *not to solve* their clients' problems.

Maintaining money making relationships with legislators. Good relationships with key lawmakers are a major marketing advantage. Close relationships with legislators are worth more to a lobbyist than any client. How, for example, does the lobbyist deal with the possibility of losing a money making relationship with a key lawmaker when the client's interests conflict with the lawmaker's interests? The temptation exists to compromise the client's interests.

Legislator-client conflicts. A legislator expects any lobbyist who is making a living from their relationship to achieve the legislator's goals just as clients expect lobbyists to achieve their goals. A client must remain alert to the possibility a legislator is pushing its lobbyist to act contrary to the client's best interests. A national government affairs manager cautions, "[Y]our agenda may require your lobbyist to go against legislators he/she is working with on another client matter, and the lobbyist may advise you to change your agenda to avoid this problem."[32]

Difficult hours. During the legislative session, work hours can be long and difficult. Lobbyists begin their days at early breakfast and end with late night suppers. Long hours take a toll after a while.

Campaign donations. A lobbyist is expected to attend fundraisers or at least send money, the lobbyist's or the clients'.

Being in all the right places. Lobbyists have to be at fish fries, golf games, pre-committee and legislative committee meetings, in the gallery, in lawmakers' offices, and in the hallways.

Negotiating. Lobbyists have to negotiate with other special interests to gain their support or minimize their opposition. Negotiations can be quite unpleasant and even hostile. Desperate lobbyists and their clients tactically use being nasty, mean spirited, dishonest, brutish, and thoroughly unpleasant to be around.

Participating in coalitions. Coalitions are the means through which most bills of any significance move into law. These are volatile associations in which each party considers at each moment the circumstances under which it quits the coalition or when it betrays other partners to advantage itself. Never knowing who might throw you *under the bus* can be stressful.

Good clients and bad clients. Some clients are delightful while others are nightmares. Because there often are more lobbyists wanting clients than there are clients wanting lobbyists, lobbyists may have to put up with wearisome personalities to run their businesses profitably.

Conflicts among clients. A lobbyist may have to resolve conflicts of interests among clients. Obviously, resolving such conflicts while keeping the fees flowing can be stressful. Clients must know potential conflicts of interest *before* hiring a lobbyist.

Managing clients' expectations and disappointments. A lobbyist has to direct clients' initial expectations and manage subsequent disappointments to continue to keep clients, even amidst what seem to be failures. A lobbyist must be good at politics, which Winston Churchill described as, "[T]he ability to foretell what is going to happen tomorrow, next week, next month and next year. And to have the ability afterwards to explain why it didn't happen."[33]

A lobbyist's diminished status with the legislature. A lobbyist may be hesitant to divulge to a potential or existing client that he or she is now on the bad side of the legislature or a particular legislator. This situation of being out of favor undermines the lobbyist's earning potential and gives a competitive advantage to another lobbyist who, for the moment, is more effective.

In short, late hours, a volatile process, competitive pressures, clients' demands, conflicts among clients, the need to obtain more clients, efforts to keep a business afloat, the necessity to build and maintain money making relationships with legislators, and so on, can place considerable pressure on lobbyists. The job can be exhilarating and very well paying, but it also can be exhausting. A lobbyist has a whole lot more to worry about than any one client.

In dealing with these pressures, a lobbyist must carefully select what to say and when to say it. Sometimes, lobbyists' efforts to protect their own self-interests may lead to a lack of openness and sincerity, at times even with their own clients.

LOBBYISTS AND CANDOR

Candor from opposing lobbyists. Lobbyists are paid to win; they are not paid to be anybody's friends. Within certain bounds, expect them to do and say whatever is necessary to achieve their clients' goals. Their behavior may seem to make little sense, but it is advancing their objectives.

The lobbyist's *duty of honesty with lawmakers* does not transfer to another lobbyist or client. Clients shouldn't take anything at face value from opposing lobbyists no matter how beguiling they may be. Don't believe their reports or their statistics or even the insider information. Check everything they say for accuracy.

A client should be suspicious if an opposing lobbyist contacts it *directly* rather than going through its contract lobbyist. To illustrate, a California lobbyist said, "I have experienced other advocates calling some of my clients to complain about me working against their bills. Luckily my clients understood that I was working for their best interests and alerted me to the situation but it basically amounted to an effort to pressure me through my pocket book which I consider about as low as you can go."[34]

Lobbyists Candor to their Own Clients. A client must consider its own lobbyist's candor in light of pressures on lobbyists described above. Some lobbying firms, therefore, may attempt to keep their clients from learning when conflicts of interests arise among their other clients and when they are having problems with lawmakers, special interests, and other players.

To foster candor clients must create with their lobbyists relationships of openness, mutual respect, and purpose. If a client can't promptly address problems with its lobbyist—and inevitably there will be problems in any significant lobbying effort—dissatisfaction will fester, the relationship will sour, and the lobbying effort will go badly.

A client should avoid making its lobbyist choose between keeping a client and telling the truth. It's the client's lobbying effort to manage. Within these constraints clients can be confident in what their lobbyists tells them.

Summary Chapter 2

A registered lobbyist gives a client an extra push by being the client's guide, eyes and ears in the capital, source of political gossip, advisor, coach, and face to the legislature. At the same time, a contract lobbyist shouldn't do for the client what the client should be doing for itself.

Lobbyists can be characterized as spectators, minor-league lobbyists, and major-league lobbyists. Any one of them may be perfectly suitable depending upon client needs. Major-league and minor-league firms each have advantages and disadvantages. Major-league firms offer immediate credibility coming from associating with their big name clients. On the other hand, small clients or clients lobbying for a single session should consider the level of priority and customer satisfaction a major-league firm is willing to give them relative to the firm's long-term, big name, and well-paying clients. Clients have less leeway negotiating fees with a prestigious firm, and the fees likely will be higher.

Being a minor-leaguer's "big client" often brings greater attention and dedication on the part of the lobbyist. For a client wanting to be the preferred client, a minor-league firm can be a perfect fit. Furthermore, a firm with fewer clients has less chance of developing conflicts of interest among its clients.

All lobbyists work under pressures, primarily the pressure to run a profitable business. Appreciating these pressures helps a client determine just how much candor it can expect from its lobbyists.

Understanding lobbyists, we now proceed to understanding lawmakers. They are the ones whose votes are being pursued.

CHAPTER 3

UNDERSTANDING LAWMAKERS

State legislatures are populated with relatively successful people, financially and professionally. Most are looking for the next steps in their professional development. A few have causes. In 2016, of the 7,382 state senators and representatives, 76 percent were male. Female legislators made up 24 percent of all lawmakers, and individual chambers ranged from 10 to 41 percent. As of 2015, the overall percent of women in legislatures had not changed for a decade.[35] Eighty-nine percent of legislators were white and 71 percent over 50 years old. In terms of demographics the average state legislator is a 56 year-old, white, Republican male.[36]

PERSONALITIES OF LAWMAKERS

A certain personality runs for political office. Most *candidates* are risk-takers with a great deal of self-confidence. Their psyches thrive in the public eye. Adulation is their life-blood. In reference to personalities and behaviors of political figures, Barron Young Smith writes,

> Many of the people willing to keep going [campaign for office] must be, in some sense, broken inside and driven to salve their emotional pain by courting the adulation of voters. Of course, there is the hunger for attention and the gaping psychological *need to be loved*. It's often been observed that electoral politics

is so demanding and unpleasant that no normal person would endure the indignities required to become a successful politician. In that sense, anyone who is willing to fundraise, glad-hand, and defend their smallest gaffes for months must derive some additional psychological benefit from politicking.[37] (emphasis mine)

In a similar vein, David Brooks states, "All politics is thymotic."[38] This phrase means politics is about legislators' *hunger for recognition*, a hunger stemming from their need for affirmation. For many politicians, a need for affirmation flows from a *need to be loved*, a topic which we will examine more closely.

Antonio Villaraigosa, former Speaker of the California Assembly, reveals, "Most of us who run for public office want to be loved and want to be popular, let's be honest."[39] New Jersey Governor Chris Christie expressed a lawmaker's need to be loved from a different angle when he said, "When you're looking for love in this job, that's when deficits get run up…When you're looking for love in this job, it's because you can't say no to anything, because someone somewhere won't love you if you do [say no]."[40]

Jim Kouri of the National Association of Chiefs of Police adds to our understanding of lawmaker personalities. He observes lawmakers have a "superficial charm" and "an exaggerated sense of self-worth, glibness, lying, lack of remorse and manipulation of others are common among politicians." He continues, "[W]hile many political leaders will deny the assessment regarding their similarities with serial killers and other career criminals, it is part of a psychopathic profile that may be used in assessing the behaviors of many officials and lawmakers at all levels of government."[41]

ELECTION CAMPAIGNS REVEAL LAWMAKERS' CHARACTERS

How candidates achieve elected office gives insight into their personalities. Steve Sutton of the Leadership Institute in Arlington, Virginia notes lawmakers are elected in campaigns that, more often than not, are driven by the "exceptionally petty."[42] Morton Blackwell, president and founder of the Leadership Institute, says, "Upon becoming a candidate, every person's IQ drops 30 points."[43] At times, political campaigns are less about issues and more about name calling, fault finding, and the missteps of each candidate.

Few voters have the time or interest to understand the majority of issues. Political advertisements generally are fast, slick, stark, shallow, oversimplified, and easily understood. Most people who receive campaign mailers stop reading after looking at the pictures and subheads. The broadcast media have even less opportunity for substance.

More often than not, candidates themselves aren't conversant on the issues. There is little time for or interest in reasoned analysis during a campaign. Most people choose their candidates at the gut level; they vote for those with whom they identify. This is especially true in this era of identity politics. "I am one of you, but my opponent is not one of us" distinctions are easier to comprehend than complex political issues that one or both candidates could not argue effectively. Superficial distinctions rather than objective facts and public policy become the focus of campaigns. Steve Sutton says that an election campaign is 60 percent appearance, 30 percent tone, and ten percent what the candidate says.[44]

Candidates surround themselves with people who make the candidate look more attractive. Their advertisements link themselves with well-known persons attractive to voters they are trying to secure. "Because political endorsements typically come from well-known groups or individuals and because they make a specific recommendation about which alternative to support, they are thought to be particularly persuasive clues."[45]

Finally, the candidate's own physical appearance can be a great asset. To illustrate, I gave a *Lobby School* to an association whose members all had at least a master's degree and a state professional license. Upon inquiring of the group as to how they chose to support one candidate over another, one woman responded, "My friends and I all vote for the good looking governor [Rick Perry]."

Once a candidate has shown how attractive he or she is, the next step is to make the opponent unattractive. The candidate goes after the opponent's negatives and weaknesses to disqualify the opponent in voters' minds.

Furthermore, lies abound in election campaigns. Although 20 states prohibit lying in an election campaign, lying is seldom prosecuted.[46]

Lies are effective because most voters don't check the facts. For example, "In Ohio, it's a crime to make false statements about your opponent in an election campaign. Still, the 2012 political season has been filled with lies, according to fact-checking organizations, including *The Plain Dealer's* PolitiFact Ohio."[47]

In primary elections candidates craft messages for their base voters, generally meaning their political party. In general elections candidates modify their images to motivate a broader range of their potential voters. In both cases, candidates promise to give *their* voters something *they* want to get *them* to the polls. They are neither concerned with non-voters nor their opponent's voters because they aren't the ones putting candidates into office.

Modern campaigning is about candidates turning out their voters and discouraging opponents' voters enough to stay home on Election Day. Few minds are changeable as to philosophy but minds are changeable as to actually voting. In his blog article "Politics 101, It's the turn-out stupid," liberal Democrat political commenter Peter Sage writes,

"There is no changing minds. But there is motivating people actually to vote..."[48]

USES OF POWER

In the capital, advocates plead, bargain, and—at times—legally bribe legislators for support. Petitioners from around the state join lobbyists and special interests seeking legislative favors. Supporters, especially those from a legislator's district, obtain special audiences. For minority party lawmakers, petitioners provide relief from feeling impotent. This can be a heady experience for many, and some legislators become "snollygosters."[49] As the first Baron Acton observed, "Power tends to corrupt and absolute power corrupts absolutely. Great men are almost always bad men, even when they exercise influence and not authority; still more when you superadd the tendency of the certainty of corruption by authority."[50]

Majority party legislators in most circumstances have more power than minority legislators do, and those in leadership have even more power than the rest of their contingent. After a while, some lawmakers begin to believe they are demigods, beliefs fueled by their own predispositions and by the people who know how to play them. Sometimes, new legislators need a year or two to realize they have become members of a "club" that, for all practical purposes, can do anything it wants. For example, the club sets its own compensation, benefits, and retirement plan. After a year or two, most legislators understand how to use their power.

Power also can be used to benefit a legislator's supporters, his or her district, and state overall. Many lawmakers have political objectives, beliefs, and values they promote. They direct state governments to serve citizens of the state through legislation and appropriations. They accomplish much good for many.

On the other hand, a legislator can use his or her power to "get back" at an opponent in his or her district or to exact revenge on a political opponent in the capitol building. A legislator may use political power to ruin the career of an opposing legislator or even to punish a member of his or her own party. Or lawmakers can abuse power to bully others into giving them what they want. To illustrate, Kenneth Ashworth recounts,

> The worst abuse of legislative power I ever witnessed was by a House member who wanted a new university in his district. His 'window of opportunity' opened when he became chairman of the House Calendars Committee, the body that schedules bills to go to the floor for final voting. He informed all House members that if they had any bills they wanted to reach the floor for passage they would have to support his bill for a new university.[51]

LAWMAKERS WANT TO KEEP THE POWER THEY HAVE AND GET MORE

Having tasted power, most legislators are motivated to keep what power they have and to procure more. They do this for both psychological and economic reasons. Once in power many lawmakers change. While I noted above *candidates* for political office are risk-takers, a political consultant reviewing this chapter says *once elected*, lawmakers are much less willing to take risks. He writes,

> I want to sort of question if not challenge...the notion that these folks [lawmakers] are risk takers. You mention this in 2-3 places and I think you are half right because they do put themselves out there for election and thus subject themselves to public approval or disapproval. However, in the same way you suggest that by the end of the first term they have learned the tricks of the trade, they have also learned small 'c' conservatism—move

slowly and in small increments, etc. i.e., Burkean conservatism of temperament (i.e., they cannot make enemies in leadership, lobby corps or constituents, etc.) Thus, I find elected officials to be quite risk averse.[52]

Some lawmakers avoid actions that could at least conceivably jeopardize their re-elections. To illustrate, "Illinois has the wrong legislature. Pols eager to curry favor with interest groups (and to get re-elected) created the Illinois debacle. Citizen-lawmakers who serve for a while and head home? Not so much in Illinois. The Capitol has too many careerists afraid to risk their cushy part-time jobs."[53] With a similar view, San Francisco Mayor Gavin Newsome remarked, "In the public sector, politicians are risk-averse. They're afraid of trying something new because they might see a bad headline the next day. That's a problem."[54]

Lobbyist Sid Rich says, "Truthfully, regardless of their public and political explanations for why they choose to serve, power is at the root of it. Power is perhaps not the main reason men and women seek public office. Perhaps it is not why they come—but it's why they stay."[55] As a result, legislators' desires to avoid losing power and to gain more power provide lobbyists with opportunities to influence them. To the degree they help legislators gain, use, and keep power, they are able to secure their support.

SOMETIMES IT'S NOT ALL ABOUT THE POWER

Some lawmakers vote for what they consider to be right and moral even against their party and their caucus. Lawmakers not addicted to power may risk their careers, even siding with the opposing party when they feel their own party is wrong and the opposing party is right on a particular issue.

To illustrate, Florida Democratic House Member Daphne Campbell represents northeastern Miami-Dade County, Florida. On April 21, 2011 Campbell, a freshman lawmaker, wife, nurse, and mother of five children, voted in support of Republican-sponsored legislation requiring ultrasounds before abortions. This was considered a pro-life vote. In response to her vote, Florida Democrat Rep. Scott Randolph, whose desk was next to her on the House chamber floor, became so infuriated a Democrat could vote pro-life he started tossing the papers on her desk, threw her pen in the trash, cursed, and ridiculed her. Her party promised she would be kicked out of office.[56] She won her next two House elections and in 2016 was elected to the Florida Senate with 75 percent of the vote. Except in the matter of abortion and family issues, Sen. Campbell remains a liberal Democrat. This is illustrated by an "F" (on an A-F scale) score from the conservative Liberty First Network.[57]

Rep. Campbell's support was meaningless to the outcome of the vote since Florida Democrats had marginal legislative power. However, she voted for that in which she strongly believed. So while my observations above as to power as motivator generally hold true, some lawmakers vote for what they consider good and right, rather than for power, caucus, or party.

Tiers of Lawmaker Power

Lawmakers fall into tiers vis-à-vis relevance to any bill. Tier 1 includes those most affecting the proposed legislation, that is, the 10 to 20 percent whose votes matter most. They are in leadership or on committees of jurisdiction over a particular bill. Tier 2 includes those who, at first glance, appear to be Tier 3 irrelevant since they are neither in leadership nor on committees of jurisdiction, but they are willing to go out of their way to help an advocate. Tier 3 includes the irrelevant 80 to 90 percent of lawmakers having little impact on a bill beyond voting *as instructed by the caucus.*

The vast majority of legislators cannot affect a particular bill one way or the other. To maximize chances of success and return on investment, advocates focus on the relatively small percent of lawmakers deciding its fate. I discuss Tier 3 and Tier 2 legislators first as they are of lesser importance, starting with the least important, Tier 3. Then I spend the rest of the chapter discussing Tier 1, the legislators to be lobbied on a specific bill.

Tier 3 Legislators. Tier 3 lawmakers' opportunity to vote on a bill is only on the floor. They vote as instructed by party leadership, meaning the outcomes of the vast majority of floor votes are predetermined by the caucus. These legislators may be quite pertinent in other areas, just not in a particular bill. They comprise 80 to 90 percent of lawmakers.

Tier 2 Legislators. A Tier 2 lawmaker is a Tier 3 lawmaker leveraging his or her membership in the exclusive club called the "legislature." This legislator is vastly more than just another co-sponsor or floor vote because this lawmaker may be able to intervene with Tier 1 lawmakers to convince them to vote a particular way. In other words, they lobby for advocates.

Tier 1 Legislators. Tier 1 lawmakers are the 10 to 20 percent affecting a specific bill. They are found on committees of jurisdiction—policy, fiscal, and procedural—and leadership, both caucus and chamber. Advocates focus on the majority party, and then court members of the minority party.

Chamber leadership may or may not need to be lobbied, depending on the temperament of the state. In a leadership driven state, one or only a few leaders need to be lobbied while in a committee driven state, all relevant committee members must be contacted. Most of the 99 state chambers, however, fall within a spectrum where lobbying leadership depends mostly upon leadership's interest in a bill. If leadership has little interest, then a lobbyist's work will be with pertinent committees.

However, in states in which I have worked, chamber leadership appoints lawmakers to committees, refers bills to specific committees, determines which bills make it to the floor, and controls floor action. This gives leadership tremendous power over the fates of bills. At a critical moment, advocates lobby leadership to intervene on behalf of their bill. To illustrate, my organization had a state Senate sponsor but no sponsor in the House of Delegates. With one of our association's members whose company was important to the state, our team called on the Speaker of the House. As a result of our visit, the Speaker instructed Delegate "X" to sponsor the bill and instructed the chamber to approve the bill. The bill became law.

The number of legislators to be lobbied varies greatly from state to state depending on the number of committees of jurisdiction, members per committee, and dominance by and discipline within the majority party. In every state, members of any committee considering a specific bill are Tier 1 lawmakers.

LAWMAKERS MAY NOT BE POWERFUL ENOUGH TO VOTE THE WAY THEY WANT

All lawmakers' ability to support anyone is limited by several factors, the first of which is the party caucus. Legislators must stay in good standing with their caucuses to have successful legislative careers. Lawmakers' votes are caucus driven, and a lawmaker crossing the caucus is stripped of his or her position or even expelled from the caucus. The stronger and more overbearing the caucus, the less freedom and the fewer choices legislators have about how they vote.

Furthermore, legislators vote in such a way as to stay in good stead with their supporters and potential supporters. Legislators generally avoid voting in ways that could upset those putting them in power and keeping them there.

A legislator is "free" to vote as he or she wishes only when the caucus is not demanding a particular vote and a vote won't result in conflict or trouble with his or her supporters. With that "freedom," the legislator factors in his or her personal politics and values, costs versus benefits, and logrolling.[58] So a petition for a lawmaker's support must run the gauntlet of the caucus, political supporters, and the lawmaker's self-interest.

SOME LAWMAKERS' VOTES ARE UNATTAINABLE

Some legislators' votes are beyond a lobbyist's reach, usually because their supporters don't like a client or the issue or the lawmaker resents the lobbyist. To illustrate, I lobbied a Democratic committee member to vote to repeal a tax on electricity used in manufacturing. I explained to him manufacturers included the state energy tax in the final cost of the product, resulting in consumers paying state tax on state tax which is bad public policy. At the end of my presentation, he said, "Bob that is the best presentation I've ever heard on why electricity used in manufacturing shouldn't be taxed. However, I will never vote your way because you aren't my people."[59] I represented manufacturing while "his people" generally opposed business interests; but he was a member of the committee of subject matter jurisdiction, so I had to try. Incidentally, our interaction was warm, so we could conceivably agree in the future on something that wouldn't cause him trouble with "his people."

Some legislators may dislike a client or a lobbyist for having supported their electoral opponents or thwarted their legislative efforts. Other legislators may agree with a lobbyist's position and like him or her personally but be prevented by their caucus from voting favorably. These legislators are not worth lobbying beyond polite introductions and making their acquaintance.

In states with polarized and solid one party control of a chamber or the legislature, lawmakers in the minority party are largely irrelevant. They may propose legislation to make philosophical or political statements or play to their supporters, but otherwise can do little.

However, lawmaking sometimes is so volatile, mercurial, and unpredictable that no legislator can be ignored. Some unexpected, highly unlikely, chamber-overturning event may take place, and the previously irrelevant lawmaker suddenly becomes central. Advocates still need to let all members and staff of relevant committees know who they are, what their bill is about, and why lawmakers should support it because, a vote is a vote.

SUMMARY CHAPTER 3

Most *candidates* for office are risk-takers thriving on adulation. Once in office, their risk-taking becomes less common because they don't want to endanger the power they have and they want to secure more power.

Lawmakers must satisfy their caucuses and their supporters to keep their seats and move into higher office. When advocates help legislators keep what power they have and gain more, legislators are more willing to help them. However, some vote for what they consider to be good and right, rather than for power, caucus, or party.

Lawmakers fall into tiers of influence: Tiers 1, 2, and 3. Advocates mostly lobby Tier 1 lawmakers because they determine the fate of their bills. Tier 2 lawmakers are those appearing irrelevant but can become quite relevant if they care about helping an advocate. Tier 3 lawmakers are the irrelevant 80 percent only voting on the floor as instructed by chamber leadership. Furthermore, lobbyists will never get some votes no matter what they do.

Advocates should not trust solely in their technical arguments, facts, and figures except when they directly relate to a lawmaker's well-being. Technical facts have little currency in deciding how legislators vote. Technical facts have a place but in themselves are seldom persuasive as we discuss in our next chapter.

CHAPTER 4

WHEN FACTS MATTER AND WHEN THEY DON'T

New lobbyists presume lawmaking is rational and that technical facts and studies are persuasive. However, in practice the value of technical facts and studies ranges from zero to critical. Zero most of the time because few in the legislature have specialized knowledge sufficient to understand the scientific, social, legal, and economic details of the myriad of complex issues facing the state with which facts and studies deal.

Occasionally technical studies do become important; not as coolly cogent tools but rather as political weapons to be used, offensively or defensively. Studies gain *critical* legislative importance when—normally in response to political attack—the legislature asks the highly educated experts employed by state executive agencies to comment on a bill's technical foundation.

Yet, a bill still needs a respectable set of facts in support; not a full blown study, just a decent set of facts. These facts do not persuade as much as give political cover to supporters backing the position.

However, at this point don't fret over the lesser importance of technical information in lawmaking. Generally lawmakers leave to state executive agencies the details of implementing legislative policy via agency rulemaking in which technical facts and studies matter greatly.

LAWMAKING IS LOGICAL BUT IRRATIONAL

The formal legislative process is logical in that it is step-by-step. A state's formal legislative procedure is found in the legislature's joint rules, chamber rules, and individual committee rules. States commonly publish their own state-specific flow charts. All bills start at the first box on the chart and those that succeed end up at the last box.

However, just because it is logical and step-by-step doesn't mean the process is technical, fact-based, or even *rational*. The making of laws is not rational in large part because legislators do not have the time, interest, or technical backgrounds to read, much less assimilate, technical materials. Lawmaking proceeds in a logical manner but within a volatile context in which most lawmakers never read the bills on which they vote, much less understand them if they do. Perhaps this is why President James Buchanan said, "Abstract propositions should not be discussed by a legislative body."[60]

THE LEGISLATIVE PROCESS IS BASED ON POLITICAL SELF-INTEREST

Politics is based on an almost, but not quite, *quid pro quo* system. "You help me, and I help you" is the primary unwritten and unspoken political rule. The exchange is never mentioned; any hint of it could be considered bribery and destroy legislators' and lobbyists' careers.

Most legislators act in their own self-interests, the interests of their important supporters, voters, and perhaps constituents. A legislator's purpose is to gain political advantage, followed by benefiting the greatest number of lawmakers in his or her party, followed by helping his or her supporters, followed by promoting the well-being of his or her district, and, finally, benefiting the state. Benjamin Franklin said, "Would you persuade, speak of Interest, not Reason."[61] The importance of technical materials can be summarized as, "Facts don't vote."[62]

BILLS STILL NEED FACTUAL SUPPORT

Although facts do not garner votes, lobbyists cannot ignore them. A bill must have a sufficiently sound technical foundation to protect supportive legislators from embarrassment and shame lawmakers who don't know the facts. Lawmakers trust lobbyists to present them with substantive bills supported by solid technical information. Buttressing is necessary so if anyone were actually to read the bill and background material, then supporting it would make good sense.

While discussing the technical side of bills with lawmakers is unlikely, advocates nevertheless need to be prepared to do so. To illustrate, I was lobbying Michigan State Senator Vern Ehlers. New to my job, I had not yet learned to thoroughly research my customer before making the sales call. Sen. Ehlers has a Ph.D. in nuclear physics from the University of California, Berkeley. He asked me extremely detailed, technical questions most people could not answer. Fortunately, I am an engineer as well as a lawyer, and I knew my technical and legal facts pretty well. Even so, he stumped me on a few questions. This example underscores the need to be prepared to answer difficult technical questions, if not from legislators, then from agencies' technical advisors.

Presenting a bad set of facts is the equivalent of lying. In a system running on trust, all it takes to destroy trust is one lie, one half-truth, one instance of "technically accurate but not totally forthright," or one failure to clear up a misunderstanding on the part of a legislator.

Ultimately, political not technical facts matter. Legislators want to know there is agreement among the parties before they decide to vote.

The most vote-getting factual testimony to a legislative committee simply is, "All parties interested in this bill agree on the draft before you." The legislative lexicon in Virginia and a few other states expresses the idea this way, "There is peace in the valley."

LEGISLATURES ARE SWAMPED WITH MORE INFORMATION THAN THEY CAN PROCESS

Of the hundreds to thousands of bills in a legislature during a four-week to six-month session, how many bills can legislators review, much less understand? Some bills are the size of small telephone books and deal with arcane topics. There is just too much information and too little time and expertise to process facts. Legislative committees at times welcome technical help. That's why they listen to lobbyists and their clients. For example, former Congressman William Clay said, "Without the information provided by business, labor and special interest group lobbyists, we could not pass legislation that does the least amount of harm to the fewest people."[63] Clients help legislators first as technical experts, and lobbyists help them primarily as political experts.

Regardless of state, lobbying materials have to help legislators. If materials don't help legislators and especially staffs do their jobs, they will have little interest in them.

Lobbyists visit the 10 to 20 percent of lawmakers who matter to them; associations flood the state legislature on their annual "Lobby Days" creating a human cacophony of teams of three to five advocates meeting with every legislator, including the irrelevant 80 to 90 percent. They hand deliver to legislators and staff white papers, kits, and brochures that are often ignored or glanced over. In addition, groups from each district visit their legislative delegation, leaving their supporting documents. Legislative offices receive letters from constituents, nonconstituents, regulatory agencies, and special interests. Major lobbying organizations prepare studies adding to the stacks. Gratuitous materials are dropped off by those thinking legislators and their staffs "ought to read" them or "might find them interesting." Other people send e-mails and faxes. The legislature is bursting with information for which there is not enough time, interest, or technical background to process.

Staff generally prefers electronically delivered information: "If you want to get your message to my boss, you better get it to me in a format I can cut and paste."[64] At the same time, however, electronic delivery makes ignoring materials easier. A member of the Florida House of Representatives told me he loves electronic communications because he goes through his inbox and deletes e-mails from everyone he doesn't know. Electronic communications allow legislators and staff to say studies or communications never arrived.

Finally, staff usually wants no more information than is absolutely necessary. A former Oregon legislative staffer once said to me, "Bob, no more than three bullet points. That's all I need." Give them what they need, no more.

TECHNICAL STUDIES AS POLITICAL TOOLS

If most legislators don't read bills, why would we think they would read supporting studies? So, what use are studies? In short, they are used as political weapons. "In politics, evidence is typically used as a weapon—mangled and used selectively to claim that it supports a politician's predetermined position that is policy-based evidence, not evidence-based policy."[65] The impact of facts depends on a legislator's bias in favor of or against a position. Favorable facts bolster and protect supporters. The same facts threaten neutral and opposing legislators for ignoring them.

In reality, technical facts are largely "media rhetoric" but don't win votes. Legislators don't need to understand technical details to enact policy into law, and most statutes lack detail for a good reason: Legislators don't want to get into the particulars for both political and technical reasons. State agencies wade into the particulars and fill in the blanks in the rulemaking process.

TECHNICAL STUDIES ARE POLITICALLY RISKY

Too much information can become politically risky. First, a study may provoke other special interests to produce rebutting studies. The flood of information may bog down the lawmaking process thereby generating hostility towards advocates and their bill; perhaps to the point both become too much trouble for the legislature to consider further.

The agency may be annoyed having to process technical matters which is better done in the "facts and law" "take all the time your need" rulemaking process rather than in the "facts don't vote" "there is too little time" politics of the legislature. A study may shift the emphasis from the political to the technical thereby giving the agency, especially a hostile one, too much influence over your bill.

Studies may produce information harmful to supporters. The media may become involved. Advocates may end up losing what control of the narrative they had.

The legislature is a policy body that likely won't be interested in or benefit from detailed technical information. Studies are not for legislatures, they are for agencies.

TECHNICAL STUDIES ARE FOR AGENCIES

Legislators and staff probably are not going to read studies. However, if it seems important enough, the legislature may ask the agency responsible for implementing a proposed law to comment on it. The agency knows if a bill becomes law, then it will have to deal with the study in rulemaking. The state's Administrative Procedure(s) Act requires the agency consider all technical information placed into the rulemaking record. By providing studies to agencies early, and if they are substantive enough, they may influence both legislative and agency lawmaking.

It is important to gain as much agency support as possible and resolve agency objections before committees of jurisdiction consider a bill. Therefore, after taking the political risk to do a study, it makes sense to give it to the appropriate agency long before giving it to the legislature. In addition, it is wise to offer the agency an opportunity for the technical experts who prepared the study to meet with agency technical experts to woo the agency to their views.

If the agency considers a study useful in advancing what the agency wants, it may recommend the study favorably to the legislature. With agency support the legislature will likely vote favorably. Legislatures seldom oppose agency *technical* recommendations.

On the other hand, if the agency opposes a bill, it is almost impossible to overcome agency opposition in the legislature, before the Governor, or in the rulemaking process. If an agency's experts read the study and tell the legislature it is flawed or worse, an advocate could be labeled a liar, credibility damaged, and, if the damage is severe enough, he or she might as well abandon the lobbying effort.

THE LOBBYIST'S ROLE IN DECIDING UPON A CLIENT'S STUDY

A lobbyist's counsel is critical to the client in determining whether or not to produce a study; and if so, to what degree of detail. Studies can be expensive and as noted above generally are quite unnecessary *legislatively*. But occasionally studies do become indispensable, especially in big legislative fights.

A good set of bullet points could be sufficient, rather than commissioning a full-blown study. Could a study be delayed until the enacted law more clearly defines study parameters appropriate for agency rulemaking? In both legislative and agency fora, will studies be unnecessary or critical? Will your study lead to the production of counter information harmful to you?

Because technical studies can be quite expensive and politically risky, a lobbyist's knowledge of the capital, key lawmakers and their staffs, agency staff, special interests, and process has significant political and economic consequences. Excessive information will be ignored for being too labor intensive to process. Less is more.

SUMMARY CHAPTER 4

Technical, legal, and economic studies have limited applicability in the legislative process. Legislators do not have the time, interest, or technical backgrounds to evaluate studies much less impartial facts. They first vote political facts, that is, the political costs-benefits to themselves.

However, lobbyists and clients must provide sound technical foundations for the actions they want lawmakers to take. This avoids embarrassing legislators down the line. Failing to reveal a bill's weak technical foundation is the same as lying. It is the lobbyist's and client's job to be honest, accurate, and credible.

While most legislators do not understand technical matters, agency staffs do. Agency expert opinions count with legislators, and their recommendations to the legislature can make or break a bill.

While most lawmakers are law abiding, some become corrupted by the capital. In our next chapter, we discuss power and corruption among legislators.

CHAPTER 5

POWER AND CORRUPTION

A major-league lobbyist declares, "Lobbying is a dance of seduction."[66] This, he explained, means effective lobbyists present to lawmakers legislative opportunities so desirable lawmakers want to do what lobbyists suggest. In this context, "seduction" means attraction to something positive. If a bill benefits the state, enhances general well-being, and helps legislators do the right thing, they are seduced by the bill, as they might be seduced by a symphony or ballet.

Of course, seduction also has an unseemly meaning. Some lobbyists appeal to legislators' baser instincts and hubris—which means excessive pride, self-confidence, or arrogance leading to a fall. Thomas Jefferson said, "Whenever a man has cast a longing eye upon offices, a rottenness begins in his conduct."[67] If "rottenness" begins as soon as a political candidate "has cast a longing eye," he or she was predisposed to corruption. While most legislators, legislative and agency staffs, Governor and staff, contract lobbyists, in-house lobbyists, and clients as described herein behave within the bounds of chamber rules and state law, advocates must remain vigilant as to the corruption flowing from power.

HAZARDS OF POWER

Power tends to corrupt, and entitlement leads to lawlessness. Unfortunately, history shows power and entitlement often weaken a person's sense of self-government and decency. Power lets people become who they truly are by removing social restraints. Joe Magee, a power researcher and professor of management at New York University says,

'Power isn't corrupting; it's freeing,'...He adds, 'What power does is that it liberates the true self to emerge...More of us walk around with all kinds of social norms; we work in groups that exert pressures on us to conform. Once you get into a position of power, then you can be whoever you are.'[68]

Edmund Burke, Irish statesman, political theorist, and philosopher, said, "All men that are ruined are ruined on the side of their natural propensities."[69] Power leads *some* legislators and *some* of their staffs to develop a sense of privilege and believe rules don't apply to them. As Nicholas Kusnetz observes, "Secrecy, corruption, and conflicts of interest pervade state government."[70]

After a time in office, some lawmakers lose their sense of moral direction. Tennessee Representative Frank Buck said, "We get to the point that we lust after power so bad, we lose a sense of what's right and wrong. I think you have a group of people in the General Assembly that lust after power so badly that they're willing to look the other way."[71]

ACQUIRED SITUATIONAL NARCISSISM

"Acquired situational narcissism," also called "situational narcissism," was first discussed by Robert B. Millman, professor of psychiatry at Cornell Medical School. He coined the term to describe the point at which, "[C]elebrities begin to share all the symptoms of severe narcissists." According to Dr. Millman, "People who aspire to stardom tend to be more narcissistic than others, but they don't develop a true narcissistic personality disorder until they begin to achieve success."[72]

Similarly, if a legislator wasn't a narcissist before being elected, he or she may develop situational narcissism in an environment in which he or she becomes well known and positioned to distribute legislative favors. As Adam Grant observes, "Power frees us from the chains of conformity."[73] In a similar point, psychologist Adam Galinsky finds, "Power psychologically protects people from influence."[74]

But power doesn't protect people from their narcissism or hubris. Those with weaker moral codes are more susceptible to the unseemly side of seduction. "[T]he psychological experience of power, although often associated with promoting self-interest, is associated with greater self-interest only in the presence of a weak moral identity" and "is associated with less self-interest in the presence of a strong moral identity…The psychological experience of power enhances moral awareness among those with a strong moral identity, yet decreases moral awareness among those with a weak moral identity."[75]

Although degrees of self-restraint and morality versus those of narcissism and arrogance vary among lawmakers, clients should be aware of the *possibility* of corruption among *a few* legislators and other players in the capital.

CRIMINAL CORRUPTION AMONG LAWMAKERS

Legislators and staffs, Governors and staffs, and executive agency officials have favors to sell, and some will sell them. Lobbyists and clients want favors, and some will buy them. Swapping favors can be done legally, and either party can initiate the transaction. However, it also can be done illegally. Most cases of misconduct by legislators are driven by greed. As George Washington said, "Few men have virtue to withstand the highest bidder."[76]

Some legislators sell favor as a perquisite of elected office, and some charge more for their influence than others. How much their influence sells for depends largely on their leadership status and committee assignments. Some committees bring in more money from special interests than others. For example, the House Committee on Transportation, responsible for billions in infrastructure dollars, is more likely to attract criminal enticements than the Ethics Committee.

Some legislators develop a sense of invulnerability because of their positions in a legislature. They may feel untouchable because their party runs the state. Some legislators consider themselves too important to go to jail while others think they will never be caught. Their expectations of not being caught may be understandable. For example, New York Speaker of the House Sheldon Silver was convicted in 2015 of taking bribes for fourteen years before he was prosecuted. (*Note: Mr. Silver's conviction was overturned in 2017 applying the McDonnell decision mentioned below. The case will be retried.*)

Although criminal conduct results in big press coverage when exposed, overt criminality is the exception. While lobbyists' corruption of legislators may be hypothesized as a lobbying technique, it seldom is proven beyond occasional revelations and scholarly speculation. Some legislators may not have strong moral codes, but they are quite aware of criminal codes, so they keep most exploitation just short of criminal. Their behavior may be unethical or unseemly, but it's not criminal.

BLURRY LINES BETWEEN CRIMINAL, UNETHICAL, AND UNSEEMLY

Differentiating among political, ethical, and criminal behaviors can be difficult. Marc Harris, former deputy chief of the public corruption and government fraud unit at the U.S. attorney's office in Los Angeles, observes, "The line between an ethical violation and a crime isn't always clear-cut, making it a challenging call for prosecutors to determine what constitutes a criminal act."[77]

The clearest line between ethical violation and crime is the link between something given to a lawmaker and an "official act." Former Virginia Governor Robert McDonnell and his wife Maureen were convicted in 2014 of exchanging official acts for compensation. However, in 2016, the United States Supreme Court unanimously reversed the convictions. "Chief Justice John G. Roberts Jr. described the former Governor's actions as 'tawdry' but agreed that instructions to the jury in his case about what constitutes 'official acts' were so broad, they could cover almost any action a public official takes."[78] Thus, the court affirmed that the unseemly and the tawdry aren't necessarily illegal.

One may question a legislator's ethics when, for example, he or she has a sudden spike in business income, gets a "sweetheart deal" on buying a piece of property or obtaining a loan, or when private organizations fly the legislator and his or her family to conferences at five-star resorts with cash allowances for food and amenities. Such arrangements may be legal or illegal.

Legislators may use their positions to steer business toward themselves, their family members, or their friends. Legislative service and riches seem to go together.[79]

Organizations may hire lawmakers as employees to protect their interests. As Nicolas Kusnetz observes, "Many of them [legislators] were involved in situations [where] they would not have had the job, they would not have kept the position, unless they were legislators. The reason why they were given the position was because someone up there thought they could do a good job for whatever industry it was."[80]

To illustrate, West Virginia Senate President Mitch Carmichael was an employee of Frontier Communications. "Frontier dismissed Carmichael in late May after he refused to torpedo a broadband internet expansion bill that the company vigorously opposed...While the bill was under consideration, Carmichael broke ranks with Frontier lobbyists.

He declined to oppose the legislation, which allowed up to 20 families or businesses to form nonprofit co-ops that provide broadband service in areas shunned by internet providers...A month after the bill became law, Carmichael received his walking papers. Frontier cited 'reduction in force' as the reason for letting Carmichael go...Carmichael said Frontier has asked him to sign a 'nondisclosure' agreement that would prohibit him from talking about his dismissal. He said he refused to sign it."[81]

While this arrangement of seemingly *buying a lawmaker* may appear suspicious if not downright unseemly, it isn't illegal. And, after being terminated he was shortly thereafter hired by Citynet, Frontier's competitor.

In a similar act of manipulation, legislators sometimes bully state agencies. Former California Assembly Speaker Willie Brown is quoted as saying, "You go back and tell those bastards that if this kid is not admitted forthwith [to UC San Francisco Medical School] without any conditions, the university's 1973-74 budget will be reduced by $10 million."[82]

Legislators may use their staffs inappropriately. For example, Michigan House Representatives, "[R]epeatedly used their staff and state resources to conduct political business, the report found. They also misused state resources for personal reasons, including having their staff lie about their whereabouts to help them cover up their sexual affair."[83]

On the other hand, just as some legislators manipulate lobbyists and their clients, so do lobbyists and clients manipulate some lawmakers. A noncriminal way to corrupt legislators and staff is to allow them to hope for obtaining well-paying lobbying jobs.

Hinting to a legislator or staffer that a job may be waiting when he or she leaves the legislature is a "gray area." Sometimes a job is just given to someone because he or she has connections as a former legislator. A former Illinois Senate staffer told me 90 percent of the Illinois legislative staff she knew would like to be lobbyists after leaving the legislature. Jack Abramoff once said he "owned" any person who hoped one day to work for him.[84] A hope of a future job may generally be a legal way of gaining legislative favor. However, any hint of *quid pro quo*, that is, the exchange of a lawmaker's support for a job upon leaving the legislature, may constitute bribery. Further, state officials—including lawmakers—exchanging "an official act" for personal benefit may constitute federal honest services fraud.

Sexual manipulation. Sex is another way of gaining favor with lawmakers. Clients, in-house lobbyists, and contract lobbyists must recognize, while quite unseemly, this is a very real part of the legislative dynamic with a *few lawmakers*. I will touch upon this just enough to inform while hopefully avoiding the salacious.

The typical legislator is a white, middle aged, financially well-off, power driven, successful male away from home for extended periods of time. Especially for males, greater power may lead to greater sexual appetite and aggressiveness: "The high testosterone levels which high political office triggers can therefore further increase sexual appetites in a politico-erotic vicious circle which can bring the most able of people to do things that their self-controlled selves would not countenance."[85] Mature female *Lobby School* participants regularly share stories about unwanted advances and ambush embraces, even about the same lawmaker.[86]

Some women are attracted to male sexual aggressiveness.[87] U.S. Secretary of State Henry Kissinger commented, "Power is the ultimate aphrodisiac."[88] Some women tolerate unwanted advances. A female lobbyist says, "If someone didn't grab your butt once a week, you were like 'What's wrong with me?' When you walk into a room, they say, 'Well our day just brightened up.' In my own judgment, you have to sort of roll with it. If you don't, you're a feminist...that no one wants to work with. You don't want to send the wrong signal."[89] (I realize some readers will find this lobbyist's view offensive, as noted below.[90]) Some rebuff advances. A mature female lobbyist says when a lawmaker's flirting is about to go over the line, she asks the lawmaker to show her pictures of his wife and children. She said that would normally "take the wind out of his sails."[91]

Some women exploit male attraction to them. "A woman lobbyist for one Governor was famous for pressing her ample bosom into the arm of a legislator as she earnestly pleaded with him to vote with the Governor."[92] A mature female lobbyist told her *Lobby School* class she and her female boss regularly give lawmakers *innocent* hugs which male lawmakers greatly welcome. Kathy Feng of California Common Cause says, "The use of sexual favors is just one more example of the tactics that energy companies and lobbyists have used to win favorable laws from lawmakers."[93]

Despite legislatures adopting sexual harassment policies and mandatory annual training, lobbyists should not presume sexual exchanges will cease. In part this may be because the drivers for the behavior remain, a few of which include: legislatures remain overwhelmingly male; acquired situational narcissism; power differential between lobbyists and lawmakers; those willing to sell and those willing to buy; sex is a proven sales technique; and some men and occasionally women are disposed to this kind of behavior.

Enough said on this unseemly topic.

Lying and self-delusion. Sometimes legislators are called liars. However, a liar *intentionally* deceives. Many well-entrenched people, including powerful legislators, are less liars than simply self-delusional. Former Governor and U.S. Senator Bob Kerrey,

[J]oked that geneticists will one day soon 'find a base pair' of genes that predisposes people to deception...And he predicted, half-seriously, that 'they'll find another base pair which say that politicians have 25 per cent more capacity for—you call it lying, I call it self-delusion...that self-delusion moment comes in a single declaratory sentence...which is, "If they just get to know me, they'll vote for me." It's just self-delusion...Some of us are good at it, and some of us are bad.'[94]

Of course, some legislators do lie. People in power generally are better at lying, perhaps because they are not worried about the consequences: "These data suggest that powerful individuals—CEOs, portfolio managers, politicians, elite athletes—don't get burned when they touch the figurative stove; they seem to be more physiologically 'prepared' to lie, which could lead to their lying more often."[95] This should not be surprising. Politics as well as sales often is based on lies and half-truths. Legislative chambers are populated by self-assured, personable, self-seeking people driven by their self-interests and working in environments tolerating such behavior.

Other legislators are not lying; they simply have their facts wrong. The distinctions between being a liar, being self-deluded, and being mistaken seem trivial, but those distinctions may be useful in understanding some legislators' behaviors.

"Playing" a client and its lobbyist. Legislators and their staffs know how to "manipulate" lobbyists whom they then expect to "manipulate" their clients. Lawmakers understand lobbyists and clients want something from them, and it is tempting for them to use clients and lobbyists to their advantage.

The expectation of campaign contributions is a given. However, some creative lawmakers see opportunities to shake down clients for more than campaign contributions. One such ploy of lawmakers manipulating lobbyists is "bell ringing."

In this scam, a legislator wants something from the lobbyist's client, so he or she introduces a bill potentially damaging the client. The bill is referred to the committee on which the legislator sits. The legislator ensures the committee chair does not bring the bill up for consideration *right away*. The legislator calls the lobbyist and says the people in his or her district do not like the client. The legislator then names a group needing a playground, service center, building, financial grant, or whatever else the lawmaker thinks he can extract from the client. Once the donation is made, the legislator "reluctantly" withdraws the bill.

The permutations or combinations of ways a few lawmakers abuse their power are many. They have learned they can more easily procure what they want by exploiting those needing their help, whether what they want is a client for their lobbyist friend, playgrounds for constituents, sex, dinners, jobs for themselves, and on and on.

However, most lawmaker shakedowns of lobbyists are for minor rewards, that is, the legislator is more interested in the restaurant or ball game than the lobbyist's issue. Or the legislator wants support for his or her favorite cause. I myself have said, "Sure senator, we can send over gifts for your charity golf tournament." Once a lobbyist allows himself or herself to become a target of easy shakedowns, legislators' expectations for gifts may never end.

CORRUPTION AMONG SENIOR LEGISLATIVE STAFF

Staffs are no more immune to corruption than are lawmakers, contract lobbyists, and clients. Staff may work criminally with lawmakers and lobbyists to secure votes.[96] They know what their lawmakers are doing including misbehavior and criminality.[97] Staff may commit crimes to help their bosses.[98] They may commit crimes to help others.[99] They may commit crimes to help themselves.[100] And staffers can be vehicles for their bosses' corruption: "The bill sailed through the Assembly without dissent and moved quickly through its initial Senate Committee only to be stalled in a second committee whose chairman refused to schedule a hearing. Finally, the Chairman's aide bluntly told the printers that for the bill to move they had to hire a specific lobbyist and pay him $30,000."[101]

Many lawmakers vote as recommended by their staffs. Staff has political intelligence and influence to sell, and that is worth money to advocates. Jason Hancock describes how staff corruption happens,

> That's especially true if legislative staffers take on corporate clients who wouldn't be required to disclose the relationship ... 'It has a corrupting influence on the process,' said John Lamping, a former Republican state senator from St. Louis County. 'When a staff member is giving a lawmaker advice on a bill or pushing for a certain outcome, it's important the public knows it is for policy reasons and not to benefit a campaign, a donor or a consulting career,' said Kevin McManus, a former Democratic state representative who currently serves on the Kansas City Council. 'Some of these staff positions are incredibly influential,' he said. 'They act as gatekeepers and trusted advisers. The question becomes, who's paying you and how do their objections impact how you do your day job in the legislature?'[102]

CORRUPTION OF THE GOVERNOR, STAFF, AND AGENCIES

For the sake of completeness and to finish the unpleasant topic of corruption, I add that Governors and their staffs and executive agencies are not immune to corruption. Governors, legislators, and their staffs are of similar personality types, and the power of their positions can trigger the same situational narcissism discussed herein.

Governors have affairs and are accused of crimes.[103] Corruption among Illinois Governors is legendary.[104] For example,

> He [Gov. Rob Blagojevich] had established a corrupt network of businessmen, political appointees, and politicians. He shook down businessmen and institutional leaders for bribes. He appointed corrupt individuals to various board and commissions to shake down hospitals, race-tracks, roadbuilders and government contractors. He is most remembered for trying to sell Barack Obama's U.S. Senate seat after Obama was elected president in 2008.[105]

Governors and their staffs engage in wrongdoing because there are things they want and they have valuable things "to sell" such as liquor and occupational licenses, state contracts, benefits, pardons, and appointments to political positions. For example, Alabama Governor Don Siegelman was convicted of selling to HealthSouth CEO Richard M. Scrushy a seat on the state board that oversaw HealthSouth.[106]

Staff can commit crime to help their bosses.[107] Governors' staffs may abuse their power such as when certain staff of New Jersey Gov. Chris Christie were charged in the 2013 closing of the George Washington Bridge.[108] And staffs may commit crime to enrich themselves. Former Gov. Andrew Cuomo staffer Joseph Percoco was "[F]ound guilty on two counts of conspiracy to commit honest-services fraud in a pair of 'pay-to-play' scams that the feds say netted him more than $300,000 from execs at two companies doing business with the state."[109]

Agencies at times act corruptly. Calling California "New Jersey West," the *Los Angeles Daily News* revealed, "[T]he president of the state's stem cell agency, the California Institute for Regenerative Medicine, Alan Trounson, took a job with a private company shortly after the institute gave the firm a $19 million grant."[110]

CORRUPTION EXISTS BUT DON'T EXPECT IT

Corruption happens *occasionally*. Normally, Governors, legislators, their staffs, and regulatory agencies honorably do the people's business. *Do not expect corruption,* but at the same time a seemingly inexplicable decision or vote may lead one to contemplate the possibility. And advocates must ensure they personally do not get caught up in the web of corruption.

POWER TESTS CHARACTER

No one in lawmaking is necessarily morally superior to another. Clients, in-house lobbyists, and contract lobbyists have their own temptations. Clients want laws to improve their bottom line and hire in-house and contract lobbyists to achieve legislative ends. In-house lobbyists want bonuses and promotions, want stature in the capitol lobbying corps, and want to keep their jobs. They can be every bit as intoxicated with and lustful for power as are legislators and contract lobbyists.

Contract lobbyists have to produce to obtain and keep clients and to justify their fees. Unfortunately, the desire for success can result in unseemly behavior. As Abraham Lincoln said, "[I]f you want to test a man's character give him power."[111]

Every person has some level of susceptibility to the seduction of power. The capital is populated with people willing to exploit and be exploited.

SUMMARY CHAPTER 5

Power brings some legislators a sense of entitlement and privilege to which lobbyists and their clients are expected to cater and to which many successful lobbyists do cater. These expectations have led to the downfall of legislators, staffs, lobbyists, and clients. A person's level of power and awareness of the marketability of that power can be used for good or ill depending on the person's moral code.

There are blurry lines among the criminal, unethical, and unseemly. Legislators may use their positions to steer business toward themselves, their family members, or their friends. They may use their positions to bully state agencies. Or they may use their staffs inappropriately.

Just as some legislators manipulate lobbyists and their clients, so do some lobbyists and clients manipulate lawmakers. A noncriminal way to corrupt legislators and staff is to allow them hope of obtaining well-paying lobbying jobs when they leave the legislature. There is a real, although small, probability you may encounter corruption in the capital.

To counter corruption, legislatures have enacted ethics laws governing the behavior of lawmakers, lobbyists, and clients. Our next chapter discusses ethics laws.

CHAPTER 6

ETHICS LAWS FOR LOBBYISTS AND CLIENTS

The Founders emphasized that virtue is necessary for the American form of government to succeed. Benjamin Franklin said, "Only a virtuous people are capable of freedom. As nations become corrupt and vicious, they have more need of masters."[112] In a similar vein, John Adams held, "We have no government armed with power capable of contending with human passions unbridled by morality and religion. Avarice, ambition, revenge, or gallantry, would break the strongest cords of our Constitution."[113] Finally, Samuel Adams noted,

> He therefore is the truest friend to the liberty of his country who tries most to promote its virtue, and who, so far as his power and influence extend, will not suffer a man to be chosen into any office of power and trust who is not a wise and virtuous man. We must not conclude merely upon a man's haranguing upon liberty, and using the charming sound, that he is fit to be trusted with the liberties of his country.[114]

Nevertheless, the lure of power affects virtue and at times corrupts some chosen to office, lobbyists, and clients. Jack Abramoff, the lobbyist convicted of mail fraud, conspiracy to bribe public officials, and tax evasion, told the Kentucky legislature, "Government is ordinary, decent people slowly accommodating themselves to a system that is rife with moral predicaments."[115] He said his legal troubles began after he lost sight of the line between right and wrong. In the end, his and the crimes of those sentenced with him added to existing distrust in government.

PEOPLE WANT TO TRUST THEIR LEADERS

Jeremy Adam Smith and Pamela Paxton focused on trust in American government saying,

> Trust is also essential to democracy, where people must be willing to place political power in the hands of their elected representatives and fellow citizens. Without trust, individuals would be unwilling to relinquish political power to those with opposing viewpoints, even for a short time. They would not believe that others will follow the rules and procedures of governance, or voluntarily hand over power after losing an election. If that trust declines, so does democracy.[116]

Nevertheless, legislators may exploit people's need to trust their leaders. We want to believe that those whom we expect to have integrity really have it. We may violently object to a legislator's politics, but we can handle that as long as we think the person is not being "bought off" by money, sex, or improper influences. Corruption among lawmakers and those who lobby them undermines the support, cooperation, trust, and virtue of the people.

NEED FOR ETHICS LAWS

Ethics laws and the rules and policy flowing from them are a legislature's attempt to teach and force good behavior, discourage unethical behavior, publicly punish and make an example of those engaging in illegal or unethical behavior, and enhance the public image of the lawmaking process.

Ethical manipulation is called *politics,* and is to be expected in any legislature. Threats, intimidation, cajoling, and enticements are natural, expected parts of the give-and-take of a political process driven by personal persuasion. For example, "Legislative leaders and the Governor amped up the arm-twisting in the hours before the vote, *negotiating side deals to entice members with projects in their districts* ... Assembly GOP leader Chad Mayes (R-Yucca Valley) pointedly accused Democrats on the fence of 'being bought off — not personally, but for your districts.'"[117] (emphasis mine)

Lobbyists' enticements include dinners, trips, and future jobs, usually as lobbyists, association executives, or government affairs directors. Some lawmakers are seduced by wanting some of a major-league lobbyist's power, connections, and especially money. Wide variations in the kinds of possible seductions mean lawmaker conduct cannot be regulated except by his or her moral compass or fear of being judged by voters.

STATE ETHICS LAWS

Each state has its own ethics regulations. While there are significant variations among the fifty states, there are also common themes. The body of ethics regulations consists of statutes, associated administrative rules, joint rules of the legislature, rules of each chamber, and guidelines of the legislature's agencies. The agency charged with enforcing ethics laws administers statutes, adopts administrative rules, and publishes guidance, including opinions on the application of laws.

Ethics laws evolve regularly, so vigilance is important. Criminal schemes are limited only by criminal creativity. They pop up like the "whack-a-mole" game: Hit a scheme in one place, and another "pops up" in another place. To illustrate, "Legislators aren't allowed to receive donations from lobbyists while the General Assembly is in session, but that law doesn't apply to legislators raising money for a federal office. And

Donovan's Connecticut staff was caught on tape conspiring to funnel money through 'straw donors' that would shield the source anyway."[118]

NONCOMPLIANCE

At the Congressional level, enforcement of lobbyist ethics law, that is laws unrelated to campaign contributions, is almost unheard of.[119] However, as discussed below at the state and even local levels the chance of vigorous enforcement of lobbyist ethics laws is quite real.[120]

Failure to comply with ethics laws can result in administrative, civil, and criminal prosecution or in a trial before the legislature itself. In most cases, the result of a minor ethics violation is a one-time forgiveness or a small penalty. In more serious cases, violations bring humiliation and loss of reputation. In egregious cases, violations may result in fines, banishment from the legislature, and even prison.

ETHICS: LOBBYIST TO LAWMAKER

The following quotation attributed to Jesse Unruh, former Speaker of the California State Assembly, describes his angst about working with lobbyists,

> This is my dilemma. If I had stayed away from the lobbyists I would have been ineffective. If I take their money and give them nothing for it, I would be a cheat. If I do their bidding, I would be cheating the public. I find myself rationalizing what I've done. The tragedy is that I may wind up serving the very elements I set out to beat—yet not even know that I have changed.[121]

Symbiotic lobbyist-lawmaker relationships can become complicated. Contract lobbyists use relationships with lawmakers to market themselves and "wow" clients with suppers or meetings with lawmakers. Lawmakers give buddy lobbyists chits to cash in for lawmakers' help. These intangible chits flow from the unspoken *not quite quid pro quo* exchange of lobbyists and lawmakers helping each other and just being friends. Some lawmakers send clients to lobbyists. Lawmakers in turn expect lobbyists whom they are enriching to provide them with campaign contributions, to control their clients, and perhaps, when those lawmakers leave the legislature, to help them secure high-paying jobs.

Ethics laws mandate lawmakers focus on the public interest rather than on lawmakers' and private interests. Using money to influence legislators is especially regulated; many states limit lobbyists when giving gifts to lawmakers and their families, either by banning the practice altogether or limiting the value of gifts.[122] These laws include not only gifts of money and valuables but also gifts of hospitality and honoraria.[123, 124] Furthermore, in some states lobbyists may neither make loans to legislators nor provide campaign contributions.[125, 126]

In addition to limiting gifts, many states restrict other influences on lawmakers. For example, some states forbid lobbyists lying to the legislature.[127] A lobbyist cannot try to influence a legislator by threatening to support the legislator's opponent.[128] These laws attempt to restrain lobbyists from influencing legislators in ways contrary to good government.

ETHICS: LOBBYIST TO CLIENT

Lobbyists have temptations and opportunities to manipulate their clients. Lobbyist to client ethics laws aim to protect clients from exploitation by lobbyists. Examples include:

Contingency fees. In 43 states contingency fees are illegal; however, lobbyists at times propose to clients contingency fees, even in covert ways. In Delaware, Louisiana, Missouri, Montana, New Hampshire, West Virginia, Wyoming, and the District of Columbia these fees are legal.

Introducing legislation to secure clients. In this scam, a lobbyist has a friendly legislator threaten or actually introduce a bill or an amendment to a bill detrimental to the group the lobbyist would like to have as a client. The lobbyist approaches the potential client offering to lobby against the bill because, being good friends with the sponsor, only he or she can save the client from the damage the bill if enacted would do to the client's interests. In their satirical article about lobbying in Annapolis, lobbyists Carol A. Arscott and Patrick E. Gonzalez write, "If you concoct a scheme to draft bogus legislation for the purpose of ginning up lobbying fees, go through the motions of having the bill introduced. You'll avoid a lot of unwelcome scrutiny this way."[129]

Overstating influence. A lobbying firm may puff its supposedly great level of influence with a legislator or say the legislator is in the firm's pocket. California law states, "No lobbyist or lobbying firm shall ... represent falsely, either directly or indirectly, that the lobbyist or the lobbying firm can control the official action of any elected state officer, legislative official, or agency official."[130]

Representing clients with conflicting interests. A state may make illegal a lobbyist representing interests that are beneficial to one client while simultaneously detrimental to another client unless the lobbyist has written releases from all the affected clients. In light of competitiveness among lobbying firms for clients a firm may be unwilling to lose either client. However, a client should avoid this kind of situation. Either the client hires another lobbying firm for representation or asks its lobbyist to contract out its work to a firm offering no conflicts. These laws are a small part of the much larger body of lobbyist-specific ethics rules designed to keep lobbyists and their clients honest and to bring a measure of integrity to the legislative system.

PROFESSIONAL LOBBYISTS' ASSOCIATIONS ETHICS

Fifteen states and New York City have associations of lobbyists dedicated to promoting professionalism among their members in particular, and lobbyists in general. A code of ethics usually is part of professionalism. These professional ethics codes deal with conflicts of interests, client communication, and candor. Some associations' ethics codes merely repeat state laws while others seek to remedy problems within the profession not regulated by state law. For example, one code states, "A member owes his client an obligation not to mislead the client. A member owes his client an obligation to correct as quickly as practically possible any incorrect information that the member has provided the client."[131]

Lobbyists' associations' rules not mirroring state law or chamber rules, have little legal significance as to protecting clients. Furthermore, even if an association's rules mirror state law, the association itself has no authority to enforce state rules. Only the state can penalize a lobbyist. An association may attempt to discipline one of its members, but it's up to the lobbyist whether to accept the association's penalty. Membership is meaningless *unless the lobbyist has been disciplined by the association.*

ETHICS: CLIENT TO LAWMAKER

Client communications with government officials influencing government action probably are legally considered to be "lobbying." A client should not presume its lobbying is under the umbrella of its contract lobbyist's registration. Generally, a client is better off registering as a lobbyist than not registering. Doing so avoids unnecessary and avoidable damage. Once registered, clients are subject to laws regarding what they can and can't do and what they have to report. They have the same duty of honesty, accuracy, and credibility as their contract lobbyists.

CLIENT TO LOBBYIST DUTIES

Clients inducing their lobbyists to violate lobbying laws can be criminally, civilly or administratively charged.[132,133] Clients violating ethics laws become less attractive clients when seeking future representation from lobbyists.

A CLIENT MAY BE LIABLE FOR THE WRONGDOING OF ITS LOBBYIST

A client may be liable for its lobbyist's bad conduct done on the client's behalf. A Washington, D.C. government litigator offers the following advice,

> Lobbying, almost by definition, involves a give and take with lawmakers that can lead us up to ethical and criminal lines that must not be crossed. As the notorious case of Jack Abramoff teaches us, the unlawful acts of a lobbyist will sometimes ensnare the clients who hired him in a spiral ending in civil and criminal liability. See, Abramoff, J., *Capitol Punishment: The Hard Truth About Washington Corruption From America's Most Notorious Lobbyist* (WNDbooks 2011). Avoiding 'capitol' consequences for the acts of your lobbyist requires you to be alert to what the law calls 'vicarious' or 'accomplice' liability.
>
> In the civil realm, 'vicarious liability' means that a principal can be held responsible for the wrongful acts of the agent. For our purposes, the lobbyist is the 'agent,' and the client, whether an individual or a corporation, is the 'principal.' A principal can be liable for civil damages or penalties even when the agent was not asked to engage in the offending conduct so long as the agent was acting within the 'scope of employment' for which he was hired. Similarly, under criminal law, 'accomplice liability' means

that when the lobbyist (agent) violates a criminal law, his client (principal) can also be charged with a crime if the client enabled or participated in that crime.

The most common consequence that can befall the unethical lobbyist's client is reputational damage to you or your organization. But in unusual cases, the client can be held liable for civil penalties and criminal violations growing out of prohibitions in lobbying certain kinds of public employees (for example, law enforcement officials or judges), or by prohibited means (for example, honoraria and gift giving). We all know giving a lawmaker cash in an envelope is obvious bribery. But less obvious is the action where the lobbyist's client is paying for trips, hotels, airfares, or small gifts to lawmakers. When the client authorizes or approves of such gifts or honoraria, both the lobbyist and his client may be charged with bribery, solicitation, or conspiracy. Paying an invoice that your lobbyist submitted to you for golf fees, airfares, or hotels of lawmakers is powerful evidence of accomplice liability. If the lobbyist's invoices are for illegal gifts, then the principal paying the invoices becomes an accomplice to an illegal activity.

Lessons that should not be learned too late include these: (1) ensure that the lobbyist's 'scope of employment' is carefully defined so that he does not have free reign to do anything on your behalf; (2) review the lobbyist's expense invoices carefully and ask questions; (3) immediately terminate the lobbyist if you discover he has planned or engaged in any unethical or unlawful course of conduct; and (4) get prompt legal advice if you suspect anything is amiss.[134]

A client is responsible for ensuring its lobbying campaign complies with the many laws regulating advocacy. It can't delegate its legal liability.

TERM LIMITS

Term limits were created in part to reduce lobbyist-lawmaker corruption by shattering the long-term, overly cozy lawmaker-lobbyist relationships stemming from lawmakers being in office too long and working over and over again with the same lobbyists. (That is, "too long" in the view of term limits proponents.) Legislators having shorter tenures should have fewer enticements because it usually takes a year or two in office to develop a sense of entitlement fully and then another term to know how to exploit lobbyists and their clients.

In supporting term limits, New York Assemblyman Michael P. Kearns says,

> The unethical and criminal acts by New York State politicians since 2000 manifestly make the case for term limits in New York State politics. More specifically, former Speaker Sheldon Silver and former Senate Majority Leader Dean Skelos abused their power and harmed the people of New York State. Term limits would have prevented this and helped New York as a state find ethical and principled leaders who look to serve others rather than themselves.[135]

Currently, fifteen states limit the number of terms an individual can serve in the legislature. In many states with term limits, legislators serve two to four terms under the so-called "eight is enough" rule. Legislators in term limit states know they are going to lose their jobs within a specified period of time.

Term limits have produced mixed results. On one hand, term limits may reduce corruption. On the other hand, term limits diminish the legislature's institutional knowledge. For example, in a term limit state, few legislators may know why an earlier legislature enacted a law. As a result, staff and lobbyists become disproportionately influential because they are the chambers' institutional memories. Further, knowledgeable senior staff may be more powerful than many legislators, especially freshmen. In contrast, the longevity of legislators in states without term limits facilitates a focus on the long-term, the creation of subject matter expertise, and the development of historical perspective.

Term limits also diminish the influence of state agencies on the legislature. New legislators do not know various agencies' legislative liaisons and may not trust agencies' advice. It takes time to know agency staff. By the time legislators decide which agency representatives they respect and trust, they have been term-limited out to be replaced by a new crop of legislators.

Term limits keep lobbyist-lawmaker relationships in a state of flux. For lobbyists, this makes business more difficult. Term limits, by design, create the need for lobbyists to rebuild relationships with legislators on a continuous basis. New legislators don't know them, so they don't necessarily trust them. This situation makes more difficult lobbyists representing clients.[136]

Finally, in states with term limits, dishonest lobbyists stay in business more easily. The memory of their dishonesty fades with each new class of legislators. A lobbyist ousted for lying may be able to return to lobbying after the legislators to whom he or she lied have been term limited out.

SUMMARY CHAPTER 6

Ethics regulations seek to restrain and channel self-interests of lawmakers, lobbyists, and clients. These laws include statutes, agency rules and guidance, the legislature's joint rules, chamber rules, and support offices' guidelines.

Because clients may be included under the state's definition of "lobby-ist" and thereby regulated, understanding the ethics laws helps clients avoid potential pitfalls. Lobbyist-to-client ethics laws protect clients from some lobbyists' schemes including contingency fees, introducing legislation to get clients, overstating influence, and representing clients with conflicting interests.

An important subset of ethics laws are campaign finance requirements. The next chapter discusses campaign contributions.

CHAPTER 7

CAMPAIGN CONTRIBUTIONS

I do not want you to think *significant* financial campaign contributions are necessary. None of the corporations and associations for which I worked *regularly* made campaign contributions. Professor Beth Leech notes, "And only about a third of the thousands of interest groups active in Washington even have a political action committee with which to give campaign contributions. The other two-thirds give zero dollars to candidates."[137] In a similar vein, Wright Andrews, former President of the American League of Lobbyists, says, "Most of the money that has influence is not political contributions but the money that is spent through lobbying, through grass roots lobbying, through newspaper advertising…That's what has influence."[138]

Nevertheless, campaign contributions are *perceived* as playing a significant role in lobbying, so in this chapter I focus upon campaign contributions of *normal amounts* of money and donating frequency. The vast majority of donors make these kinds of contributions; and of which I'm personally familiar. At the end of this chapter I refer to a report on the influence *large donations* have upon lawmakers, a subject on which I have no direct experience.

At the same time, don't think campaign contributions have no *potential* benefits. However, before clients make donations that can win them *marginal* leverage with lawmakers or result in *severe* political damage to themselves, they need to think about "why" and "with whom" and "how much" and "is this *really* what I want to be doing?"

PERCEPTIONS AND REALITIES

Former California Assembly Speaker Jesse Unruh said, "Money is the mother's milk of politics."[139] The public believes campaign donations influence legislators' votes; that may or may not be true, as discussed below.[140]

Research shows lawmakers "win" in several ways by getting donations. However, contributors, on average, don't "win" much by making donations. Data provided by The National Institute on Money in State Politics demonstrate political candidates for state political offices who spend *significantly* more money than their challengers win more often.[141] Professor Leech observes, "Dozens of studies have discovered that, on average, organizations that give more campaign contributions succeed in their policy goals *no more often than we would expect from mere chance.*"[142] (emphasis mine)

How important are cash campaign contributions to achieving legislative goals? What do campaign dollar contributions actually "buy" for the donor? Can nonfinancial contributions be as effective as money? Let me start with what I consider to be three campaign donation realties.

Reality 1: Money doesn't change legislators' votes. When deciding how to vote, legislators have more important things to think about than campaign contributions. A few include:

> Lawmakers first satisfy the people putting and keeping them in office, namely supporters, voters, and to a lesser degree constituents. They are not going to abandon voters for donors.

> Lawmakers do not vote contrary to their caucus, party, and instructions from chamber leadership. To do so could ruin their careers. They will take donations but won't respond with votes.

Next, legislators don't change long-held political values for money. Were they to do so, opponents would call them "flip-floppers," and nobody likes a political flip-flopper.

Incumbent legislators have earned political interest group ratings. They are not going to endanger these ratings for donations, especially since these ratings impact the support received from entire subsets of donors. To illustrate the importance of ratings a lobbyist writes,

> [A]dvocates who lobby for associations or other large groups publish election 'scorecards' and assign elected officials grades based on how they vote. For example, the Chamber of Commerce publishes a scorecard that assigns every Representative and Senator a grade based on how supportive each elected official is of businesses. Lobbyists for these groups will often use the scorecard as leverage to entice legislators to vote for or against major pieces of legislation. Over the course of each legislative session, the Chamber will announce that votes on several major pieces of legislation are 'scorecard bills' and recommend that legislators either vote yes or no in order to receive a good grade on their scorecard that is published annually after each legislative session.

> The Chamber scorecard carries considerable influence considering the fact that many businesses and corporations will use the scorecard to determine which candidates to send campaign contributions. National groups such as Freedom Works, the NRA, and Heritage Foundation also utilize their own Scorecards as leverage when lobbying members of Congress.[143]

A lawmaker receives thousands of donations from thousands of contributors. Unless the contribution is extraordinarily large, a donation won't have much impact, or get much notice beyond getting the donor on an e-mail list and on the elections commissions website.

Money is just one form of campaign contribution. Others types of donations, which can be as effective as money, if not more so, are discussed below in "Effective Campaign Contributions Don't Have to Be Financial."

Reality 2: Legislators' needs are as much emotional as financial. People under stress need friends, and campaigns are stressful. Therefore, most politicians' deeper needs are beyond money. Their primary needs are personal including witnessing friendship, and getting and keeping love, admiration, and power.

When a legislator receives a meaningful campaign contribution, he or she "feels the love." Contributions affirm lawmakers; a lack of donations makes them feel rejected. A manager of many election campaigns adds, "Pols loved to be loved. When they get donations, it boosts their ego and confirms their candidacy. The opposite is also true ... Candidates live for money and watch every penny every day."[144]

Reality 3: Votes don't follow money; money follows votes. This has been stated by many commenters. "The strongest studies supporting the reform cause suggested only a modest influence for money, an influence far weaker than other factors affecting a lawmaker's vote. Even studies that showed some effect seemed biased by endogeneity.[145] In other words, legislative votes might attract money rather than be the result of a contribution."[146]

If money isn't going to procure votes, then why do some interest groups give so much money to campaigns? They give money because they don't have anything better to give; money is all they've got. They can't give candidates what they need, and that is votes. Professor Alan Rosenthal says, "Interest groups with individual members may be able to deliver voters to a candidate but most organized groups—in particular corporations, businesses, and professions—cannot deliver votes. But they can deliver dollars; and they do so to the best of their ability, for a number of reasons."[147] Money helps lawmakers feel donors' support and money given to them is money presumably *not given* to their opponents. The fewer the number of votes special interests can deliver, the more money they need to give to influence lawmakers.

SIGNIFICANT CAMPAIGN CONTRIBUTIONS "BUY" A MEASURE OF POLITICAL BENEFIT

The particular amount of money constituting *significant* varies among the states. A *significant* financial campaign contribution:

Buys an increment of influence for in-state clients. Influence levels range from great to nil. A candidate's friends and family members have significant influence, followed by donating supporters who are affected by proposed legislation. Last among the many other influencers are nonconstituents who are in-state, unaffected, noncontributing, and nonsupporting. A contribution raises a donor's level of influence.

A client with no presence in the state should not expect much from its donations. While candidates welcome their money, my experience was they also didn't expect it. During my entire lobbying career working in many states, only once did a state lawmaker ask me for a donation. I didn't make it, and my bill still became law. However, a client's out-of-state donation may help its lobbyist gain a measure of influence from which the client benefits, at least indirectly.

Enhances a voter's influence. Money is no match for grassroots, but it boosts a voter's influence with his or her lawmaker. A meaningful donation moves a voter up to the next level of influence to become a supporter. In-state but out-of-district *substantial* contributors realize a net increment of influence, although less than that of a donor-voter.

Says a client is on the legislator's team. I once overheard a Florida Senate committee chair "dialing for dollars" asking potential campaign contributors, "Are you going to be on the team this year?" He didn't ask for an amount; he just asked them to be on his "team." Lawmakers are more interested in knowing who is there for them than the size of the donation.

Says the donor is not on the opponent's team. Candidates want to know that contributors love *them and them alone* and not their opponents. If a donor gives to opponents, each will take its money, but neither will like or trust the donor or be there for him or her in the future. This is because both know that the donor is not a friend but is merely hedging bets. Former U.S. Senator Slade Gorton says, "It just seems to me that those who were trying to buy influence on both sides were simply wasting their money…The idea that you can play both sides and have people like you, or influence them, I think is an extremely foolish one."[148]

Inclines legislators to help donors *on the margins*. A donation may motivate a legislator to help in ways that cost him or her little. Professor Alan Rosenthal writes,

> A campaign contribution can make a difference where there is no obvious public interest, where the legislator's own values and beliefs don't come into play, and where the legislator's party has no position…campaign contributions do make a difference when the visibility of the issue is low; when the issue is narrow, specialized or technical; when the issue is nonpartisan or non-ideological; when the public is indifferent, divided or ignorant; or when no opposition exits.[149]

Relieves legislators from asking for money. For *some* candidates, "dialing for dollars" is an unpleasant and demeaning task, and large donations reduce the amount of time the candidate needs to spend asking for money. To illustrate, former Congressman and current MSNBC personality Joe Scarborough referring to his two annual NRCC [*National Republican Congressional Committee*] fundraising events said, "But it's something I absolutely despised. There are people you talk to two times a year, and it was when you were having your two events. They knew why you were calling, and you know it just sort of felt dirty. Some people I suppose can do it and feel no shame about it, but it's a very ugly process."[150] Helping candidates avoid unpleasantness may earn some measure of gratitude.

Encourages candidates. On the other hand, *some* candidates enjoy asking for money because large donations uplift them emotionally and affirm their campaigns. They feel the love when they count the money.

Motivates lawmakers to help resolve conflicts among donors. Legislators do not want to choose among large donors. Rather than alienating any, a legislator may choose none. The lawmaker may instruct them to work out problems among themselves and even mediate conflicts.

Shows donors understand the process. Making *significant* campaign contributions demonstrates an understanding of the political process and capital culture. Exhibiting such understanding can result in an increment of respect from lawmakers and special interests.

Establishes capital players. An organization making significant contributions, even if only to a small number of legislators, is seen as a "player" in the capital, even if a smaller one. For now note that *significant* is a relative term depending on the state, with the well-off expected to give more and the less well-off expected to give less.

BUYING ACCESS

However, while money doesn't get votes, it buys *access* to lawmakers. So where do you buy access? Do more dollars buy more access, or is there a minimum amount to gain it? Can access motivate a legislator to do anything *meaningful* that he or she wouldn't do otherwise? If not, then what good is access?

Buying *general* access to lawmakers starts with fundraisers, meet-and-greet receptions, and other group events. The next level of access is somewhat more selective and includes leadership conferences such as the nonpartisan National Conference of State Legislatures and the Council of State Governments; and the partisan American Legislative Exchange Council, national and state party committees, and political action committee events. More privileged access is developed at legislative retreats and party caucus meetings.

The top level of access is semiprivate: golf outing, fishing trip, or hunting getaway. The amount of attention received at any of the above is directly proportional to the benefit brought to legislators.

Individual legislators give private access for contributions because they have to give at least something to keep donors giving. Thus, a donation can help supporters secure face time with legislators in their legislative offices as well as at private dinners, ball games, and other places.

But are donations necessary to get a nice visit? Bradford Fitch reveals,

> There's a dirty secret in Washington that neither Congress nor the special interest community want out: Campaign contributions really don't influence legislative outcomes all that much. The reality is that a campaign contributor will likely get access to a legislator, such as getting a phone call returned by a member of Congress or his senior staff. However, the average constituent

can get the same access with about the same amount of effort, such as by showing up at a town hall meeting, or getting three or four fellow constituents with similar interests to set up an in-person meeting in the legislator's Washington or state office.[151]

Constituents should expect that lawmakers' doors are open to them. And for voters or supporters, the welcome mat is out. For non-constituents, I have found that most lawmakers or their staffs will see those who *demonstrate that what they are selling is good for the lawmaker, district, party, etc.*

ACCESS IS MORE ABOUT IMAGE THAN GETTING VOTES

While access to an individual lawmaker may be somewhat overrated as to influencing votes, access may have a big winner, and that winner is the lobbyist cultivating business. Access is marketable, most notably to impressionable clients. It gives clients a "wow" and a feeling their lobbying fees are being well spent. So on one hand, campaign contributions really don't influence legislative outcomes all that much while on the other hand, access is exciting, and clients will pay for it.

However, *in moving a bill into law,* a lobbyist who can mobilize a legislator's supporters, donors, and constituents; maximize special interest consensus; minimize controversy; and gain the support of legislative staff and executive agencies is more valuable than a lobbyist who is "wowing" clients with access. Lobbyists not invited on fishing trips and who can't sell access, nevertheless, can win their clients' issues—even without campaign contributions.

HOW CANDIDATES SPEND CAMPAIGN DOLLARS

Although misappropriation of campaign funds happens occasionally, most legislators are not going to spend campaign contributions on

Rolex watches and lavish lifestyles. They have better ways to spend donations, a few of which include:

Increase voter support. Legislators know voters can take away their jobs; with job loss, they lose power and income, and their self-worth may diminish. A manager of many legislative campaigns says, "If a candidate loses, it *will* diminish their ego. I have known people to go on antidepressants and stay indoors for 2-3 months."[152] (emphasis in original) Solid voter support gives lawmakers more secure positions and longevity in the legislature, which in turn can lead to better positions in the chamber and caucus and can propel lawmakers to even more important political offices.

Buy opposition research. Opposition research discovers every objectionable thing an opponent has done or said over the course of his or her entire lifetime. As a campaign consultant notes,

> It is expensive as all get out and sometimes PIs [private investigators] are used. They dig into everything including listening to committee tapes and/or transcripts so that they can use votes out of context (i.e., a meaningless committee vote as opposed to a floor vote on the final draft later). [Name of state party] hires pros and has in-house people too and spends a bundle. They also use trackers [spies] to go to every event the opponent does.[153]

Build political war chests. If an incumbent's high probability of re-election isn't enough to discourage a rival, then a large campaign war chest may do so.

Purchase positions from the caucus. Legislators use campaign contributions to "purchase" support from their party's caucus to gain better committee assignments, committee chairmanships, ranking positions, or positions in chamber leadership and in the caucus. "Increasingly in Congress, and in some state legislatures, leadership positions and committee chairmanships require substantial amounts of caucus fundraising."[154]

The more influential the position, the more campaign money it costs. Former U.S. Rep. Bob Ney said, "I was directly told, 'You want to be chairman of House Administration, you want to continue to be chairman.' They would actually put in writing that you have to raise $150,000. They still do that — Democrats and Republicans. If you want to be on this committee, it can cost you $50,000 or $100,000 — you have to raise that money in most cases."[155]

Lawmakers purchase leadership positions and better committee assignments because these positions have more power and attract more donations. In turn, caucuses redistribute the money to caucus members and thereby advancing the party.

Purchase support directly from fellow lawmakers. A lawmaker may purchase support directly from party members. An expert in the flow of political money comments,

> 'Leadership funds' [PAC money] are used to transfer money from special interests to those vying to become speaker, who then in turn generously spreads it around to people who may vote for them for speaker ... or they can do independent expenditures, etc. This has the effect of ingratiating the new rep or newly re-elected rep to leadership and also essentially allows any interest group to give double the amount allowed by law.[156]

And if the lawmaker doesn't win re-election, the political debts accrued from spreading money around might help the now ex-lawmaker obtain a job with a lobbying firm.

CAMPAIGN FINANCE LAWS

Campaign finance laws vary among states, and a coherent discussion I leave to other authors. However, I will touch upon a couple of aspects.

Three-quarters of the states prohibit corporate and union contributions to candidates' election campaigns. For this reason, organizations solicit voluntary campaign contributions from their members to aggregate into funds from which political donations are made. The broad title for these organizations is *political action committee* (PAC). PACs direct money to candidates believed to be favorable to the organization and its members.

Advocates also donate to organizations whose functions lawmakers attend. The money doesn't go directly to elected officials but to organizations that advance party or lawmakers' interests.

Federal law prohibits 501(c)(3) IRC charities from making financial contributions to candidates. Twenty-nine states limit campaign contributions during the legislative session and in fourteen, lobbyists are prohibited from making campaign contributions.

Unprincipled clients may try to circumvent statutory limitations on corporate and union contributions by paying their lobbyists inflated fees with the expectation excess monies will be used for campaign contributions. Circumventing the law is called crime. Crime is punishable by fines or prison time or both for clients and contract lobbyists.

Clients and lobbyists have a duty not to lead legislators into ethical trouble. Illegal campaign contributions harm election campaigns through negative press, having to return donations, drawing unwanted scrutiny by the elections commission, and giving ammunition to the candidate's opponent.

MAKING CAMPAIGN CONTRIBUTIONS IS RISKY BUSINESS

Legislators are looking for "friends" as much as they are looking for money. By giving to opposing candidates, a donor reveals to lawmakers he or she is the friend of neither; the candidates will take the money but distrust the donor.

If a donor is a political liability, the lawmaker may take the money and then say he or she doesn't even know the giver—which may or may not be true. U.S. Sen. Joe Manchin represents a pro-gun state. When questioned about taking $87,000 from gun-control law firm Paul, Weis, Sen. Manchin said, "I know it's hard to believe and I know it's hard for people too, [but] I don't have any idea who gives me money. I don't solicit from the standpoint of, 'If you do this for me,' quid quo pro, that's never been me. That's not my political mantra at all."[157]

State elections commissions report on who gives how much to whom. Reports let legislators distinguish the faithful from those hedging their bets. Therefore, donors have to ask themselves whether or not they want to gamble their political capital on an election, and if they do, do they bet on a "long shot" (generally the challenger, with an overall 5 percent chance of winning) or the "odds-on" favorite (generally the incumbent, with an overall 95 percent chance of winning)?

If the long shot wins, the donor is rewarded with a return on the wager but with payoff limitations mentioned earlier, especially Reality 1: Money doesn't change legislators' votes. But if their candidate loses, the donor will be on the winning legislator's list of enemies, and this can have long-term negative consequences. Never underestimate a lawmaker's petulance and desire for revenge. For example, a legislator may refuse to support a bill or may work against a donor who supported his or her opponent(s) in the past.

Clients should expect that if they win, they win little. But if they lose, then they lose big.

"SMART" MONEY GOES TO INCUMBENTS

The smart money goes to incumbents in part because voters need a big reason to fire someone they elected just two or four years ago. Increasingly, incumbents are re-elected without opposition. Smart money goes to lawmakers in the majority. Donating to the minority risks alienating the majority, and the majority generally determines the fate of legislation. Furthermore, in many states the minority party is for all practical purposes irrelevant to the lawmaking process. For example, as of this writing the Hawaii Senate has zero Republicans, and the Wyoming Senate has three Democrats out of a total of 30 senators.

Generally, advocates should not donate to statewide campaigns such as Governor, attorney general, commissioners of state agencies, and state offices. These officials have little influence on the legislature's disposition of bills. I recommend donating to people who can actually affect a specific bill.

THE CAMPAIGN GIVING SEASON

The more assured of re-election, the less a lawmaker needs to solicit support. This is because support is showered upon legislators by those betting on a "sure thing" or those terrified of the challenger winning. The showering of support can lead lawmakers to presuming their reelection.

To illustrate, newly elected Tennessee state Senator Carol Rice explained that she, a Republican in what at the time was a very Democratic state, won her challenge to an incumbent because—according to Sen. Rice—her well-entrenched opponent just presumed that he would win his election, so he largely ignored her until too late. While she had little money, she worked hard, even campaigning at garbage dumps, and to the shock of all she won.

During the campaign giving season, facts matter as little as ever. A legislator looking for support is inclined to take the time to hear about a donor's issue and why it is good for the legislator, district, and the state. But I feel these visits are more for donor-lawmaker bonding than about lawmakers learning, much less remembering, the details of what another donor needs.

Do not use donations to try to force legislators to take a stand on an issue. Any hint of tying support to a vote is not only unseemly but potentially is criminal bribery. Even if criminal charges are not forthcoming, should a lawmaker's position suggest a hint of *quid pro quo*, both donor and the candidate face serious political damage.

CAMPAIGN FUNDRAISERS

Whether to attend a fundraiser is determined by how much the client needs the legislator, and how much the legislator needs the client. Reasons for attending include:

Obtaining face time with the legislator. If the donation is large or if attendance is poor, a donor might be able to speak to the legislator. However, if the fundraiser is well-attended or the donation insubstantial, the legislator probably won't recall the donor was there.

Showing player status. To those few who may notice, a donor's participation suggests the donor is a "player."

Hearing gossip. Donors share gossip and "talk shop" with other clients and their lobbyists. They may find who is "in" and who is "out" with leadership, what groups are working what bills, and other things that can help achieve their legislative goal.

Identifying the legislator's other supporters. Donors may have opportunity to establish some level of camaraderie with the legislator's other supporters. This may help in building coalitions or generating support for a bill.

Developing professional contacts. Finally, donors may find themselves speaking to people at the fundraiser who have little interest in the candidate but are there to develop their own professional contacts. "Sometimes they want to mix and mingle and network with the other guests who are far more important to their business than a mere candidate."[158]

A Good Name May Be More Valuable Than Money

Having a representative of a respected organization at a fundraiser is more prized than dollars. Legislators want to be linked with organizations enjoying voter goodwill. Few lawmakers will exclude a donor with a valued name who offers to pay an amount less than the suggested donation. To illustrate, the spokesperson for a liberal public interest group wanted to attend a Democratic candidate's fundraiser, but the suggested donation was beyond her ability to pay; so she asked me what she should do. I told her to go to the fundraiser and ask to attend for fifty dollars; if the likely inexperienced staff refused her, then she should request to speak to the campaign manager. This is exactly what happened. When the campaign manager concluded that her group's name on their contributor list was more valuable than the suggested contribution, he promptly let her in.

Effective Campaign Contributions Don't Have to Be Financial

Other forms of campaign contributions are more tasteful than money and every bit as effective, if not more so. For the candidate, the purpose of a campaign contribution is to help win an election; the donor's purpose is to improve its relationship with the candidate. Nonmonetary contributions accomplishing both include:

Endorsements. Support from groups held in high regard by voters is valuable. Those who like the endorsing organization hear the message "this is the candidate to bet on." For new candidates, their first endorsement is the hardest to secure for which they remain grateful.

Plaques and awards. A plaque proclaiming a candidate as "person of the year" is valuable for campaign literature. State ethics laws may limit the amount of money that can be spent on a plaque or award.

Sympathy. Empathy, sympathy, and emotional support in a campaign create a bond between donor and lawmaker that transcends money.

Media support. A favorable letter to the editor or buying an advertisement praising and thanking the lawmaker uplifts the lawmaker and legitimates the candidate to the general public.

Working on a campaign. Donors who share a common experience by working on a campaign develop a bond with a lawmaker. This may bring future influence. Be advised a 501(c)(3) IRC regulated charity sending campaign workers representing it or appearing to do so may endanger its tax exempt status.

Letting the legislator be seen. Lawmakers love to speak to organizations, tour facilities, and participate in "show and tell" opportunities. To illustrate, my principal's bill was in trouble, and I needed our district's Tier 3 liberal Democrat to intervene on our behalf with a Tier 1 liberal Democrat. I wanted to give her a campaign contribution. However, my corporate officers had little connection to her. While my principal's unionized workers supported her, for reasons of internal politics I couldn't ask them for help. So, without management or union involvement, how could I make a donation?

The answer was I invited her to the factory to stand at the entry/exit turnstile during shift change. At shift change, union workers were coming in, and union people—her people—were going out. She looked into the faces of those who would benefit from her help and who would help her. She obtained more advantage from waving to and greeting her supporters than she would have gained from a substantial financial donation. And afterwards she persuaded her Tier 1 sister lawmaker to support my principal's bill which later became law.

Nonmonetary support may be more meaningful for "showing the love" to a legislator than cold cash (of course, *both* are better). And for the donor, it's good because nonmonetary contributions need not be stated on campaign finance reports, thereby somewhat insulating it from other lawmakers finding out what was done and reacting emotionally.

Contributions Show Donors' "Love"

Alan Rosenthal identifies eight benefits from campaign contributions; he lists the primary benefit as keeping friends in office so they can do friendly things for supporters.[159] "Friends helping friends" is not far from my perspective that donations build warm relationships with lawmakers with whom clients can be friends; while making the relationship with estranged lawmakers a little less tense.

Contribute with integrity, not to seduce. Build the relationship before giving, and then give in accord with the intimacy of that relationship. I say this realizing some lawmakers will never want rapport, but the relationship can be improved. Civil relationships are in all parties' interests, and neither client nor the lawmaker knows when they might unexpectedly agree. If a client operates in a lawmaker's district, building relationships is easier and more natural. The best giving is not dollars but showing respect and interest in the well-being of the lawmaker.

Significant campaign contributions go to *friendly* lawmakers. With *opposing* lawmakers, nonmonetary contributions such as visits to facilities, lets them know given the right circumstances and on an *ad hoc* basis, a client could be on the lawmaker's team. With a friendly lawmaker, this *rapprochement* is easy; but even with a hostile lawmaker an open attitude still bears fruit.

INFLUENCE OF BIG MONEY ON LAWMAKERS

Do bigger donations buy more access? Former U.S. Sen. David Durenberger said, "The size of the contribution makes little difference in terms of access. Support is the key ingredient. Members realize that companies cannot contribute equally, but that small contributors are often as important as large ones."[160] Sen. Durenberger's observation is consonant with a theme of this book—lawmakers are looking for love and votes from the home-folk more than they are concerned with dollar amounts.

However, other lawmakers say organizations making *unlimited donations* run lawmaking in the United States. Jon Schwarz offers a number of comments from lawmakers supporting this view in his article, "'Yes, We're Corrupt' A List of Politicians Admitting that Money Controls Politics."[161] A comment in his article from former U.S. Rep. John Dingell well summarizes its theme,

> Allowing people and corporate interest groups and others to spend an *unlimited amount of unidentified money* has enabled certain individuals to swing any and all elections, whether they are congressional, federal, local, state … Unfortunately and rarely are these people having goals which are in line with those of the general public. History well shows that there is a very selfish game that's going on and that our government has largely been put up for sale. (emphasis mine)

The operative phrase here is *unlimited amount of unidentified money.* To place the above in the context of *normal* lobbying and donations, the following describes my interaction with Rep. Dingell.

I wanted Rep. Dingell as a Tier 1 lawmaker to support my bill which was before the U.S. House Commerce Committee on which he served. Michigan earlier had passed a similar favorable state law for which I lobbied over three years to enact. His son Chris Dingell, then a Michigan state Senator, was a deciding favorable vote.

Rep. Dingell was in Ohio raising money for an Ohio Democrat. Ohio is a state in which my principal had significate presence. I bundled campaign contributions from my corporate officers sizeable enough to be admitted to a limited attendance reception with him. I spoke directly to him about our bill, but he opposed it as much after we made the donation as before. In other words, the sizeable amount of bundled money we gave and access we received had no influence on Rep. Dingell's vote.

This suggests in the course of normal lobbying neither standard amount donations nor access have much influence on a lawmaker's vote. So while big money may indeed impact *some* lawmakers that level of donation is not part of ordinary lobbying.

SUMMARY CHAPTER 7

Making campaign contributions is a major decision. As long as clients realize they are not going to get anything dramatic for their campaign dollar and donating to anyone other than a "sure thing" is risky, they and their contract lobbyist can plan a campaign giving strategy.

Because legislators' votes are not going to change—no matter how large the donation—and access is overrated, dollar campaign contributions should play a small part in a legislative campaign. However, if all a donor has to give is cash, then of course give the maximum allowed by law; on the other hand, if it can deliver votes, then give modestly to add its name to the "team" roster, that is, the campaign finance report.

Campaign contributions involve both risks and benefits. Donate to keep a friendly lawmaker in office or somebody else out of office. Money follows votes; votes don't follow money.

The following chapters discuss whom to lobby in order of importance: special interests, legislative staff, executive agencies, legislators, and the Governor. We begin with lobbying special interests.

CHAPTER 8

LOBBYING SPECIAL INTERESTS AND COALITIONS

A special interest is any entity working to influence government decision making. Special interests include individuals, governments, corporations, churches, labor unions, charitable organizations, associations, or groups of organizations sharing a common interest. What today we call special interests the Founders called "factions." In a free society unions of common interests are inevitable. Don Wolfensberger writes,

> [James Madison] defined a faction as a group of citizens 'united and actuated by some common impulse of passion, or of interest, adverse to the rights of other citizens, or to the permanent and aggregate interests of the community.' The danger lay not in the existence of parties or factions, but in the prospect that one or more would become a majority faction that would adversely affect the rights of minorities and of property. The duty of government was not only to protect the rights of citizens to fully develop their differing faculties, but then to regulate the resulting factions so that they did not do harm to others: 'The regulation of these various and interfering interests forms the principal task of modern legislation and involves the spirit of party and faction in the necessary and ordinary operations of government.'[162]

To those outside of the lobbying world, the term *special interest* carries a pejorative political connotation when contrasted with *public interest*. However, the term *public interest* is itself nebulous because in reality a purported public interest is almost always some group's *special interest*.

What Special Interests Do

Special interests are the most influential force in effecting a bill. They and the coalitions they form drive the capitol and the capital. They write most bills, maximize consensus and minimize controversy among players, line up bill sponsors and co-sponsors, provide talking points to lobbyists and legislators, work bills through committees, obtain and keep votes, lobby the Governor's office as necessary, and participate in executive agency rulemaking to implement legislation. Special interests capture, focus, and direct lawmakers' supporters, voters, and constituents, including other interest groups, as discussed below. After their home-folk are taken care of, lawmakers are almost exclusively motivated by the special interests that help to put and keep them in office.

Special interests are critical to a lawmaker's success. They offer lawmakers support and lawmakers help them gain favorable laws. As long as there is no hint of *quid pro quo,* all of this is perfectly legal and is the currency of participatory lawmaking. By providing sound technical, legal, and economic foundations, special interests enable lawmakers to vote their own best interests and those of the public. However, at times lawmakers' personal best interests conflict with the public's apparent best interest.

Lobbying Allies and Opponents

Special interests are allies and opponents, and both must be lobbied. Special interests that would benefit, should a bill become law, are a bill's allies, and those harmed are opponents. Of course, what constitutes "benefit" and "harm" is in the eye of the beholder, and each special interest does its own cost-benefit analysis in terms of investment of time, treasure, and political capital versus payoff. A special interest's level of involvement with a bill depends on how important it is relative to other bills it is lobbying.

Lawmakers expect opponents to have spoken to each other before talking to lawmakers, and to represent accurately each other's views to lawmakers and staff. Conversations among potential allies and opponents help establish a roster of potential coalition partners.

COALITIONS AGGREGATE, APPLY, AND CONTROL POWER

Coalitions present themselves to the legislature as a united constituency of substantially affected parties focusing their technical expertise and political power on a particular issue. Coalitions are informal or formal, small or large, *ad hoc* or permanent. An informal coalition may consist of a few organizations just talking, especially when the issue is relatively small in the scheme of the legislative session and the organizations' own legislative priorities. These likely are *ad hoc* and have no name or identifier; participants' expenses are borne individually, and joint expenditures, if any, are funded in a kind of a relaxed "passing of the hat."

Formal coalitions, on the other hand, have an official name, listed members, organizational structure, officers, assignment of duties, budget, and often professional staffs; they may hire lobbyists and other consultants. If there is a continued need for them, they incorporate into permanent associations. An incorporated coalition that lobbies must register as a principal.

An *ideal* coalition brings together *all the special interests* affecting a bill. The first goal of a coalition is to maximize consensus and minimize controversy among all interested parties. President Lyndon Baines Johnson in his ever-earthy manner said, when referring to his rival J. Edgar Hoover, "It's probably better to have him inside the tent pissing out, than outside the tent pissing in."[163] The second goal is to apply aggregated political strength to the matter at hand. The third goal is to control coalition members; bringing them into the same tent increases political strength and keeps them from undermining the lobbying campaign.

COALITIONS EXIST FOR ADVANTAGE, NOT LOVE, LOYALTY, OR DEBT[164]

Coalitions exist for advantage, not love, loyalty, or debt. Do not presume that any group will be either an ally or an opponent. Charles Dudley Warner said, "Politics makes strange bedfellows."

Expected allies may become enemies on a particular issue; and *expected* opponents become allies. To illustrate the unpredictability of who might be a coalition partner or an enemy, a Washington, D.C. contract lobbyist writes,

> I was calling a top lobbyist at another company, somewhat confused by the other company's advocacy against our campaign to get a certain bad law changed, even though the other company would also benefit.
>
> Me: 'Hey, you guys are putting out the word that the [name of legislation] bill treats my company differently than yours, that we get exempt, and that you get screwed. That's incorrect and I'm happy to explain it.'
>
> Other company VP: 'We know that.'
>
> Me: 'Oh, so will you guys stop lobbying against the bill?'
>
> Other company VP: 'No.'
>
> Me: 'What?'

Other company VP: 'We're against the bill because it helps you.'

Lessons: Politics is based upon guesswork over the emotional responses of people; 'political science' is not a true science. The actions and reactions of others are not predictable because even if you can predict the effects of a given policy upon another, other factors may be controlling. In my story, the other company was being obnoxious but they weren't being stupid…the policy change we sought would have opened up a huge market for my company, but it was not a realistic opportunity for the other company.[165]

In this case even being in the same industry impacted by the same bill didn't necessarily translate into intra-interest group issue commonality. This is because *coalitions exist for advantage, not love, loyalty, or debt*; thereby making unpredictable and fickle alliances. Being so, they are also filled with intrigue, sidebar deals, and the reality that any moment they may throw a coalition partner under the bus as soon as advantage ends; just as the coalition partner would throw them under the bus.

HOLDING A COALITION TOGETHER

Special interests, legislators, agencies, and the Governor's office may be arranging sidebar deals with coalition partners to try to entice them away from the coalition. If the sidebar deals are good enough, coalition partner(s) may be more than willing to walk away from the coalition. This "divorce" happens because, for one or more partner(s), the benefits of the coalition have ended while the drain in time, money, and political capital continues.

A coalition member should ask this question: *What amendments to the bill will cause me to quit the coalition?* Next it must answer: *What amendments will prompt my coalition partners to "throw me under the bus?"* No matter how agreeable, charming, and collegial, coalition partners seem, they are asking themselves these same cost-benefit questions. When the advantage ends, so does membership in the coalition.

LEGISLATURES EXPECT CONSISTENCY FROM COALITIONS

Legislators expect consistent messages from a coalition. When a coalition brings to the legislature an agreement into which coalition members freely entered, legislators presume consensus to continue at least until such time as the foundation for the original agreement no longer exists. Legislatures expect special interest predictability and order.

Legislators don't like surprises. They don't want to have to redo their own political calculus because a coalition changed its mind. The shortness of many legislative sessions does not provide sufficient time to respond to sudden modifications in coalition positions. Although lawmaking itself is capricious, and deals are being cut all the time, a coalition should not change a stated position without an extremely good political reason. Changing position leads to the perception the coalition and its members are inconsistent and unstable and therefore untrustworthy; so any change in position, policy, or lobbyist should occur only if absolutely necessary.

Of course, legislators and other special interests understand coalition partners are not married for life. Everyone knows a coalition is a temporary connection based on one particular bill or issue, and partners are free to oppose coalition partners on other bills.

ANTITRUST ISSUES

When *marketplace competitors* gather, they have to be aware of antitrust restrictions. Should competitors joining forces affect the marketplace, intentionally or unintentionally, they could find themselves under legal scrutiny from regulators. If any conceivable antitrust claim could be leveled against it, then with advice of counsel, it should preemptively adopt a formal antitrust policy which clearly states nothing it does or discusses should be construed as collaboration to illegally affect trade, the marketplace, or competition.

Coalitions should be safe legally as long as their discussions are limited to the legislature, its common effect on them and those similarly situated, and how to deal with politics. Legal counsel ensures discussions and actions don't stray into anti-trust territory.

SUMMARY CHAPTER 8

Special interests write bills, develop consensuses, line up votes, and otherwise drive the process of lawmaking. After their district supporters and voters, legislators are almost exclusively motivated by the special interests that put and keep them in power.

Special interests unite into informal and formal coalitions because a single principal seldom can push a substantive bill to enactment on its own. Informal coalitions tend to be small and work on bills of narrow interest. Formal coalitions have membership rosters, officers, assignment of duties, and greater power.

Coalitions exist for advantage. They are ephemeral unions. Every thoughtful member of a coalition calculates, *What can cause me to quit the coalition?* and *What will provoke my fellow coalition members to "throw me under the bus?"*

After special interests, legislative staff is the second greatest influence in enacting a bill. They are the topic of the next chapter.

CHAPTER 9

LOBBYING LEGISLATIVE STAFF

A Florida House member said, "Win my staff and you win me."[166] Because of their ability to sway, legislative staff is the second most influential force in enacting a bill.

STAFF LEVELS VARY AMONG STATES

In 2015 there were 31,678 state legislative staff members, 26,631 permanent and 5,547 session staff. Individual states vary considerably with regard to numbers of legislative employees with numbers ranging from a few dozen permanent chamber staff in North Dakota to thousands of permanent chamber staff in California.

Larger states have well-paid, permanent, professional, subject matter specialist, partisan and nonpartisan staff. Smaller states have permanent, professional, nonpartisan staff. One state legislative chamber provides its members with personal support staff while its sister chamber provides none. In one state, partisan personnel serve on committees; in another state, nonpartisan personnel staff committees; in yet another state, the party caucus provides committee staff.

STAFF CAN RUN THE LEGISLATURE

Full-time legislative staff can *functionally* run the legislature, and in most cases, they do. Upon resigning to become a lobbyist, California State Senator Michael Rubio said, "In my absence, Senate staff will remain in the district and Capitol offices to respond to the needs of residents of the 16th State Senate District—as they have always done."[167] Lawmakers delegate to trusted staff some lawmaker duties. For example, staff members have been known to cast votes for absent legislators on the chamber floor. New Jersey Senator Bob Smith said, "It is perfectly permissible to have your aide vote your conscience."[168] Staffs know their bosses' politics, the districts' needs, key voters and donors, legislators, the caucuses, and *skeletons in the closet*.

TYPES OF LEGISLATIVE STAFFS[169]

I discuss four sets of legislative staffs: chamber, committee, caucus, and personal. Each set has junior and senior members, partisan and nonpartisan.

Chamber staffs. Chamber staffs are nonpartisan; that is, they are chamber functionaries operating the infrastructure. They do not engage in politics, and it would be a grave mistake to try to enlist any of them in *political* efforts. Chamber positions include:

1. Legislative Council;
2. Legislative Counsel;
3. Legislative Legal/Bill Drafting Services;
4. House Clerk and staff;
5. Senate Secretary and staff;
6. Bill room;

7.   Sergeants at Arms; and

8.   Parliamentarian.

These professionals provide continuity of chamber operation. They generally have long careers in the legislature. They are not focal points of most lobbying. Although chamber staffs can be as arbitrary, capricious, and petty as anyone else (particularly if their bosses are), such behaviors are the exception. The vast majority of chamber staffs are professional.

Chamber staffs' expertise and knowledge of process, politics, and current state of the law are invaluable. To illustrate, a lobbyist says,

> [Chamber] Staff can help you and your legislator avoid pitfalls in the legislative process. Our senator was helping us get an amendment that would uniquely qualify us, and not our out-of-state competitors, for grant programs that were being authorized in a bill. We drafted an amendment citing a provision of tax code that affected us but not the other organizations. Legislative counsel said that if we cited tax code, the bill had to go through the Ways and Means Committee, which would cause heartburn for the bill's sponsors and not make our freshman senator any friends among leadership. Instead, they rewrote the amendment using words from the tax code without actually citing it. The amendment passed cleanly, 'without objection.' Then we pointed out the amendment to our supporters in the agency. They simply pasted the language into their next request for applications, which brought the provision to the attention of the agency's legal reviewers. Ever since, the same language has appeared in all of the agency's RFAs [Requests for Authorization], and we've won numerous grants because of it.[170]

Committee staffs. Depending on the state, committee staffs are either nonpartisan or partisan. Smaller states having relatively fewer staff provide nonpartisan, professional, clerical, and legal support. Larger states have greater numbers of staff who are partisan and professional providing clerical, administrative, legal, and technical support.

Partisan committee staffs are ministerial *and* political. Politics is part of their job. They advance the interests of the majority party including the committee chair and committee majority. Although paid by the legislature they are hired by and serve at the pleasure of the committee chair. In the interests of a well-functioning committee, they also assist the committee minority.

Large state committee staffs tend to be legal and technical specialists and have senior ranking because committees demand greater experience and technical knowledge. They have sufficient technical expertise to interface with executive agency experts. Committee staffs tend to have longer terms in the legislature because committee staffs overall won't change unless the majority changes.

All staffs evaluate the technical elements of bills; however, partisan staffers also consider politics. They translate technical input from agencies and special interests into formats understandable and useful to legislative committees. They also ensure advocates' facts do not embarrass committee members. Committee staffs protect legislators from being tricked technically and politically.

Committee staffs heavily influence the chairs and committee members. To illustrate the power of committee staffs, consider the committee's bill scheduler. He or she generally works for the committee chair. If a bill is not scheduled, then normally it is dead. While in small states all bills tend to be scheduled, the sheer volume of bills in larger states results in committees taking up relatively few. I am personally acquainted with large state committee bill scheduling rates as low as 25 percent, meaning 75 percent of referred bills are never considered by the committee because they aren't scheduled. Some committees exist for the purpose of killing bills by reporting none.[171]

A former scheduler for the chairman of a legislative committee said to his *Lobby School* class, "He [the committee chair] entrusted to me the scheduling of bills for committee consideration. When special interests would complain to the chair about my failure to schedule their bills, he would tell the complainers to take it up with me. He supported me in all my bill scheduling."

A scheduler may choose not to calendar a bill because it would take too much staff energy to process. Or the politics may be such that it might consume a disproportionate amount of committee time. Some of the most important staff lobbying focuses on getting a bill scheduled followed by regularly checking with the scheduler to make sure a bill stays on the committee schedule.

Caucus staffs. Each party's caucus has its own staff. Of course, caucus staffs are thoroughly partisan. The larger the state, the more independent the caucus and caucus staff are from legislative oversight.

Caucus staffs may receive more attention from lobbyists than do many rank-and-file legislators because caucus staffs draft bills, do legislative research, make policy and voting recommendations to caucus members, develop strategies to move legislation, and shepherd bills through the legislative process. They do the thinking necessary to inform and support caucus decisions. In limited circumstances, they may fulfill some legislators' duties such as requesting amendments.

Personal staffs. In larger states, legislators have personal staffs. These range from a half-time shared secretary to fully staffed capitol and district offices. In mid-sized states, personal staffs tend to be junior; and their jobs may be the first ones they have held in the legislature. In larger states, personal staffs may include senior members, especially for important legislators. Expect full-time personal staffs to be partisan; that is, they reflect their bosses' political values. These staffs are lobbying focal points because they advise their bosses about whom to support and how to vote.

Staffs are so important to directing their member's vote that an advocate should not be disappointed never meeting with the legislator; or if a visit with the legislator is short and without substance. A legislator may be vitally interested in few bills during the entire session although he or she votes on dozens, if not hundreds. The legislator's staff guides him or her in voting on all bills but especially on the ones the he or she has not been able to follow. If both *personal and committee* staffs support a bill, the likelihood of getting the lawmaker's vote greatly increases. Personal staffs protect their bosses' credibility. They may not have the technical expertise of committee staffs, but they have access to agency experts, trusted special interests, and committee staffs.

Personal staffs assist their bosses with constituent matters. They may represent legislators at district events and help constituents deal with state government. They know key supporters, voters, and constituents; they are close to the "constituent pulse"; and they know the local political gossip, all of which are important in advising their bosses. Upon the lawmaker leaving the legislature, their insider knowledge makes them ready to run for the office their boss has vacated, thereby offering the district political continuity in the capitol.

Senior staff. Senior staffs have expertise, longevity, or both. Partisan senior staffs work for caucuses, chamber leadership, committees, and well-entrenched legislators. Unless intentionally positioning themselves to obtain lobbying jobs, they remain in the legislature because they love the process and benefits. And when they leave the legislature, lobbying jobs may await them.

In many state legislatures, senior staffs are among the highest paid state employees, and they and all legislative staff may receive benefits, such as raises, when other state employees receive nothing. Unlike other state agencies, the legislature has its own hiring and promoting practices and sets staff salaries and benefits.

Senior staffs have heavy influence with their legislators and more influence on legislation than most freshmen lawmakers. Senior staffs may serve as legislators' *alter egos*. For example, in larger states lawmakers may delegate bill related negotiations to their staffs. To illustrate, several lobbyists and senior legislative staff met to resolve issues over my principal's bill. One senior staffer told us, "I have the authority to commit my member's vote at this meeting." I had no reason to doubt his claim. Nor did I doubt that other senior legislative staffs in the meeting had similar authority, although no others said it.

Senior staffs serve as a legislatures' institutional memory for several reasons. In 15 states term limits erode legislators' institutional memory. Because senior staff know more than their bosses (especially new legislators) about chamber rules, legislative history, other legislators, other legislative and agency staffs, lobbyists, special interests, who among a legislator's constituents matter, and the legislative process in general, senior staff have profound influence on their legislators' politics and votes.

Junior staff. Junior staffs tend to be either personal or junior committee staffs. They often have short careers in the legislature, or they rotate among legislators until they move to more secure committee assignments or are hired by entrenched legislators. They influence the views of senior staffs because neither legislators nor senior staffs have the time or interest to meet with every advocate. That job at times may be left to junior staffs.

Partisan staff. Partisan staffs are motivated by priorities set by their legislators and caucus. Advocates are no more going to convert them to a new way of thinking than they are going to change their bosses' views. Politics rule. They want to protect their legislators' and committee chairs' credibility and advance their legislators' and their own careers. They also are motivated by politics and facts, and they have little time for amateurs.

Nonpartisan staff. Nonpartisan staffs are protected from external political pressures. If chamber leadership is doing a good job, nonpartisan staffs don't care if a lobbyist is a drinking buddy of the chamber leader. In fact, some chamber rules prohibit lobbyists from even entering staffs' offices. They can invite advocates to speak with them to clarify something about a bill, or a legislator may ask staff to talk to a lobbyist. The invitation has to come from them. A lobbyist who lies to staff to procure an audience with them can be formally banned from their offices.

Session staff. Most state legislatures hire some part-time staff support whose employment lasts the duration of the legislative session. They are called "session staff" and generally serve as clerical or personal staffs. In some states, session staffs may outnumber permanent staffs by 50 to 200 percent. Like all legislative employees they have no civil service protections and can be fired *at will* by chamber leadership.

Useful Information. Staff welcomes information that helps them do their jobs. If advocates' materials don't help staff do their jobs, they will have little interest in them. At the same time, too much information is not welcome. A former staffer and now lead lobbyist for a trade group told his *Lobby School* class, "When a bill would come up for a vote, my boss would ask me: 'Who was for the bill? Who was against the bill? How much did it cost? Who is the lead sponsor?'" Because many lawmakers first vote politics, that's pretty much all they want to know.

Staffs don't know the special interest intra-political currents and appreciate learning from lobbyists what may come their way. A former staffer noted, "I've had many different experiences with lobbyists during my career at the Florida Legislature—some good and some bad. I would say that my best experiences have come at times when lobbyists have come to legislative staff with a 'heads up' on various issues of importance coming before the Legislature."[172]

When staff wants unbiased information, they request the relevant executive agency to review and comment on materials received. If they don't want to know more, they may "lose" or ignore the study and supporting materials.

DISRESPECT FOR THE ILL-INFORMED

Disrespect for the ill-informed is a major motivator of lawmakers and especially staff. They welcome anyone who can help them do their jobs well. The ill-informed cannot help them do their jobs.

Failure to "run the traps"[173] may be the most fundamental proof someone is ill-informed and an amateur. When I worked in Washington, D.C., a staffer inquiring as to whether a lobbyist had done his or her job thoroughly, would simply ask, "Did you run the traps?" For example, if a staffer asked an advocate what a relevant interest group thought and the advocate replied, "I haven't spoken to that interest group," then by not running the traps the advocate showed him- or herself to be ill-informed. A staffer or lawmaker, upon hearing the inadequate reply, may tune-out or terminate the lobbying visit as a waste of his or her time.

ALL STAFF ARE IMPORTANT

Just as "There is no little enemy," there is no unimportant staff. If staffers don't like the lobbyist they may not return his or her calls or e-mails. They may ignore advocates whom they don't respect or find annoying. Nevertheless, under any scenario, advocates must treat them with great respect and defer to their considerable power.

A staff person's support may not be critical, but opposition can be fatal. Rudeness to a staffer may cause a legislator to think his or her office has been disrespected. Former U.S. Sen. Mark Hatfield said, "I have a familial relationship with my staff, anyone who abuses them starts with a minus position with me. Some people who abuse staff are polite and gracious to the Member; I dislike that double standard. Abusing my staff is like abusing my family."[174]

Staffers often feel underappreciated, overlooked, and overworked. Although some have great power, they also have great job frustrations including shortages of staff because of retirement or job changes or staff reductions; the need to train junior staff who may or may not remain on the job very long; budget cuts; legislators who do not appreciate them; public cynicism about government; partisanship and incivility on the job; and competition for jobs. They work under great pressure.

Friendly staff can be invaluable to advocates such as by scheduling a bill for committee consideration; telling them about gossip, occasional scandals, and what their opponents are saying; giving a "heads up" on committee business and caucus activities; putting their communications at the top of a legislator's inbox; and adding to their credibility. Most of the time staffs can mean the difference between success and failure.

Being a staffer has great thrills and challenges, and staffs have their own agendas and personal desires for professional advancement. They may want to keep their current jobs or secure better ones in the legislature. Many want to become lobbyists. Unlike other state employees they don't have job security, or civil service protections, and they are hired and fired at the whim of legislators. The next election may see them unemployed if their member is voted out or retires. And finally, they can be every bit as intoxicated with power, self-important, narcissistic, and subject to corruption as lawmakers.

SUMMARY CHAPTER 9

Legislative staffs are the foundation of the lawmaking process. In larger states, staff can be more important than legislators. This chapter discussed four types of legislative staffs: chamber, committee, caucus, and personal. There is no such thing as unimportant staff. *A staff person's support may not be necessary, but his or her opposition can be fatal.*

Legislators and legislative staff rarely act contrary to the advice of the technical experts who work at state agencies. The next chapter discusses the third most important influence on a bill becoming law, that is, the executive agency.

CHAPTER 10

LOBBYING EXECUTIVE AGENCIES

Agencies are the third most important influence in moving a bill to statute. This is because, *for all practical purposes*, they are technical staff to the legislature. In Chapter 13, *Executive Agency Rulemaking, Appeal, and Enforcement* you may find answers there to questions that may arise here. But for now, I want to focus on just one aspect of agencies, namely they are major players in the legislature.

OVERVIEW OF AGENCIES

Agencies exist to implement statutory and at times constitutional laws. Legislatures create most agencies; voters create a few through voter initiatives. Most agencies are located within the executive branch to help the Governor faithfully execute the legislature's instructions as found in statutes and the budget. Former Illinois Governor Dan Walker said, "Most of the people in the state of Illinois, and I think this is true across the country, are much more affected in their daily lives by operation of the administrative and executive part of government than they are by 90 percent of the bills [of] the General Assembly."[175] Other terms for agencies among many include administration, authority, board, bureau, commission, council, department, district, division, and office.

AGENCIES ARE POWERFUL LEGISLATIVE PLAYERS

Agencies are powerful in the legislature for a variety of reasons, including:

1. Legislators listen to them;

2. Special interests fear them;

3. Governors protect them;

4. They "veto" bills;

5. They introduce legislation;

6. They employ in-house lobbyists; and

7. They lobby.

Legislators listen to agencies. As the legislature's *de facto* technical staff, legislators give great weight to agency advice and recommendations regarding *substantive* legislation, as contrasted with budget requests. Few legislators have the technical expertise to evaluate, much less challenge, agency experts who often hold advanced degrees in the field under discussion in the bill.

Special interests fear agencies. Agencies impact special interests because agency approval improves chances of bill passage while agency opposition generally dooms a bill. Next, to implement legislation, an agency adopts highly detailed rules. Agency rules can take away everything the legislature gave a special interest or give that interest more than the legislature would give.

Further, special interests when considering opposing the agency, as a matter of self-defense, generally weigh the threat and burden of agency retaliation. Therefore, special interests seriously consider what an agency wants as they strive to stay off the agency's "bad side."

Governors protect agencies. Governors employ agencies to assist them in executing the legislature's directions and accomplishing the Governors' goals. Legislative interference with agencies can lead to a constitutional separation of powers battle. Veto messages regularly read, in essence, "Since you lawmakers meddled with (or ignored) my agency—'BILL VETOED.'"

Agencies "veto" enrolled bills. In the unlikely event the agency didn't kill a bill in the legislature; agencies can "veto" the enrolled bill and statute. They do this in a couple of ways.

First, when Governors receive enrolled bills they ask agencies what to do with them. The agency can urge the Governor to veto an enrolled bill based on technical facts, the cost to the state of implementing the law, the difficulty of implementing the law, the effect the law would have on the state government and other agencies, the impact the law would have on the public, any hint of violation of separation of powers, or a combination of these things. Expect the Governor to do as recommended.

Second, if the Governor doesn't veto the enrolled bill, it becomes a statute. However, an agency for all practical purposes can "veto" a statute by not implementing it either through failure to enter into rulemaking, or by not enforcing the rules it does adopt. The net result is until rulemaking is completed, there isn't a law; and nobody knows what the law means until the agency says what it means, as explained in its adopted rules. Furthermore, if the agency won't enforce its rules for reasons of policy, interest, or resources, for all practical purposes the law is without effect.

Agencies introduce legislation. Agencies introduce legislation using several vehicles which differ in substance and frequency from state to state. Depending on the state, they may introduce bills automatically without a sponsor or the Governor's approval, use legislative bill slots reserved for agency and Governor's bills, or employ surrogate constituent groups to introduce legislation for them.

Agencies' in-house lobbyists lobby. Agencies lobby for what they want, propose and oppose legislation, work with and threaten special interests, build coalitions, negotiate bill language, and are extremely influential legislative players. Accordingly, agencies have their own lobbyists who, being political, have much broader policy perspectives than the fact-and-law career civil service technical staffs. They can influence the agency's policy makers to support or oppose a bill.

However, influencing an agency on legislative matters may be considered to be lobbying the agency. Lobbying the agency may require registration as an agency lobbyist; even getting a second lobbying license and complying with a second set of ethics rules. Florida offers an instructive example,

> [A]lthough properly registered in the Legislature, the lobbyist may not be correspondingly registered in the executive branch for the same principal. This is a gray area; but since the lobbyist is now attempting to influence the outcome of a legislative measure within the state agency, it is highly recommended that the lobbyist become immediately registered within the executive branch notwithstanding the issue being a legislative public policy matter.[176]

AGENCY INFLUENCERS

The following influence an agency's legislative position:

1. Special interests;
2. Stakeholders;

3. Public employee unions;

4. Agency lobbyists and political appointees, and perhaps technical staff; and

5. Governor's office.

Special interests. Agency special interest supporters, often kindred spirits, benefit from favorable agency actions including infusions of state money or having interests intersecting with an agency's goals. Agency special interest opponents are generally those losing money or influence.

Stakeholders. Stakeholders are agency regulated organizations and a subset of special interests. They may influence an agency by providing technical information, mobilizing constituents and coalitions, influencing the legislature, and having legal standing and economic resources to challenge the agency, either administratively or judicially. However, given agency regulatory and enforcement power over stakeholders, most tread carefully when dealing with agencies.

Public employee unions. Public employee unions and agencies are natural allies because both want the agency to have more public money and employees. To illustrate, the government affairs director of a public employees union told me his union collaborates with agencies to move more money and employees into agencies, minimize budget and personnel cuts, and add more agency programs. For example, his union lobbied the state's department of corrections to include more personnel in its budget requests. The union then coordinated its lobbying with the agency's lobbyists, and with other special interests that would be enriched by more state money going to corrections. By working together, the agency and the union were successful. The agency acquired more public money and hired more employees, and the public employees union gained more members.[177]

Agency lobbyists and political appointees. Agency lobbyists often have the ear of political appointees placed at the highest levels in agencies to carry out the Governor's agenda. Political appointees have authority to set agency legislative positions, including supporting or opposing a bill.

Governor's office. The Governor's chief role in legislation is preparing the state budget. Agencies are vitally interested in persuading the Governor to include their wish-lists in the Governor's proposed budget. This in turn gives the Governor at least some nominal influence with the agency. However, a Governor's office may or may not involve itself significantly in non-budget related legislation.

The Governor appoints, or nominates subject to Senate approval, agency top management. This gives him or her influence with the agency's political appointees. However, the Governor may or may not have any influence with agency career civil service staff, especially those protected by public employee unions. To illustrate, I was among a group of lobbyists meeting with staff of a state Department of Environmental Conservation (DEC) in a state known for its powerful public employee unions. A new Governor had just been elected. The senior DEC director at the meeting announced to our group, "We here at the DEC don't like [full name of new Governor]. We are going to sit on our hands for the next four years until [full name of new Governor] goes away." Staff was confident that given civil service and union protections they without consequence could ignore the Governor and his appointees. So, depending on how much an agency's civil service staff likes the Governor and the strength of civil service and union shielding, the Governor and political appointees may or may not influence career civil service staff.

Finally, an agency is motivated by its budget, mission statement, strategic plan, and enabling legislation. Legislative appropriations, as found in the budget, are the agency's lifeblood, financially enabling it to exist and to carry out its duties. An agency's mission statement describes what the agency exists to do, such as protect the elderly, collect revenue for the state, educate children, and so on. Its strategic plan, which is designed to implement both its mission and the enabling legislation, is normally quite detailed and covers a span of five to ten years. Enabling legislation is the statutory obligation and authority the legislature gives to an agency. Agencies are motivated by those who help them achieve their strategic plan.

AN AGENCY MAY UNDERMINE ITSELF WITH LAWMAKERS

Legislatures normally do what agencies recommend. However, if lawmakers feel the agency disrespected them, they may chastise the agency just for spite by cutting its budget, reducing its authority, or voting against it. To illustrate, the committee of subject matter jurisdiction *repeatedly* asked the agency for comments on my principal's bill. The agency *repeatedly* ignored the legislature's pleas for advice. The committee finally called up my bill for a final vote. As was normal procedure, the agency was invited to testify on all bills, including mine. The agency strongly objected to my bill. I feared my bill, after years of work, was going to die given agency hostility.

However, much to my surprise, a committee member who generally supported the agency said to the committee, "We have for over a year repeatedly asked [name of agency] for its comments on this bill, and they for a year have ignored this committee. I propose that we in turn today ignore everything [name of agency] has said today about this bill." The committee did just that, and then favorably reported my bill which became law. My principal was the unexpected beneficiary of a political fight seemingly flowing from agency disrespect for the legislature.

SUMMARY CHAPTER 10

Agencies serve as technical staffs to the legislature, and lawmakers normally do what the agency recommends regarding *substantive* legislation. This means an agency can greatly help a bill or kill it. The Governor likely will do whatever the agency recommends, including vetoing a bill. Like every interest group, an agency is influenced by those helping it achieve what it wants. Its legislative allies are organizations relying on public money, public employee unions, and special interests whose goals coincide with the agency's. We discuss agencies more in Chapter 13, *Executive Agencies Rulemaking, Appeal, and Enforcement.*

Having considered special interests, legislative staff, and agencies, our next chapter discusses lobbying legislators.

CHAPTER 11

LOBBYING LEGISLATORS

Although legislators are fourth in *political* importance, *constitutionally* no one else matters because they alone vote on bills. All lobbying of special interests, legislative staff, agencies, and perhaps the Governor's office, has been done for the moment when the first committee of jurisdiction takes up a bill. Starting with this committee—and then with each succeeding vote—clients and lobbyists sequentially learn whether they have failed or if they have hope for the next steps.

ROLES OF THE LEGISLATURE

While the roles of the legislature are many, "Passing a state spending plan is the legislature's single most important job."[178] Next, it enacts general law to incorporate public and private interests into law. Either the budget or general legislation carry a bill to statute.

The budget. No legislation is more certain to pass than the budget. The legislature uses it to:

1. Fund government;

2. Express state policy;

3. Influence the courts;

4. Direct the Governor and executive agencies; and

5. Enact temporary substantive law.

Fund government. Through the budget the legislature allocates the state's financial resources among thousands of competing spending priorities. Government shuts down without funding. The main budget bill may be hundreds of detailed pages with supplemental budget bills adding more. However, unlike the federal government, state budgets must balance in all states except Vermont.[179] This means state legislatures often make difficult tradeoffs in setting the budget.[180]

Express state policy. Expressing state policy, the legislature uses the budget to favor some groups[181] and disfavor others[182] thereby emphasizing, "The budget is not just a collection of numbers, but an expression of our values and aspirations."[183]

Influence the courts. By reducing or increasing funding for the courts the legislature conveys the extent and direction lawmakers prefer judges to have. "It goes without saying that those courts that are well-regarded within their own states are more likely to escape the budget axe."[184]

Direct the Governor and executive agencies. The legislature directs the Governor and state agencies through line-item appropriations. It can effectively repeal a law or reverse agency action by defunding agency implementation of a law or activity.[185] That is, the law remains on the books, but since the agency has no money to implement it, the net result is for all practical purposes the law has been repealed. In addition, the legislature may use the budget process to force the agency to do something a particular lawmaker wants.[186] It can reduce an agency's budget to show its displeasure.

Enact temporary substantive law. The budget is the only bill not subject to the common state constitutional requirement that a bill relate to a "single subject,"[187] and it is the only bill that must be enacted.[188] This makes the budget a potential vehicle for enacting legislation that would not otherwise pass as stand-alone *general* bills. Enactment of law by budget is done using budget riders; rider-enacted laws continue in effect until the next budget.

Limits on using the budget to pressure the governor, agencies, and the courts. The legislature's ability to pressure the other two branches *broadly* or *drastically* through the budget is more bluster than reality. "Revenge" reductions and refusals to fund fully the Governor's and agencies' projects are legislative pressure tactics. However, their impacts are more on the margins rather than anything profound. This is because the legislature—and perhaps the state constitution—gives agencies and judges specific duties to perform; and for them to do so, the legislature must appropriate sufficient money. In practice, as cash flow permits, the vast majority of last year's budgeted items are carried over into this year's budget at pretty much the same amount of funding.

And even if the budget isn't passed on time, the money to keep government working keeps flowing despite whatever crisis might exist. To illustrate, "As the new year began in Illinois, there was still seemingly no resolution in sight to a months-old problem: The state had no budget. But even without one in place, many parts of Illinois government continued to operate, as the result of a mix of judicial, legislative and executive actions."[189]

General legislation. Legislatures enact general laws impacting virtually every aspect of society. Chapter 1 outlined the formal process for enacting general laws which is the normal path for a bill. Much of a legislative session is devoted to this standard process of lawmaking, including committee hearings, public testimony, lobbying by special interests and executive agencies, and so on. In a typical legislature, thousands of bills are introduced, and a few dozen to hundreds of single-subject general laws are enacted each session.

RULES FOR SELLING A BILL

Former Congressman Tony Coelho said, "Lobbying is like any other business; it is selling, selling, selling yourself and your product."[190] Six maxims guide legislative sales:

1. Nobody cares until you make them care;

2. Politics trumps policy;

3. Follow the money;

4. Customers buy to meet their needs, not yours;

5. "Lobbying is a dance of seduction;" and

6. "People don't like to be sold, but they love to buy."[191]

Nobody cares until you make them care. In light of the thousands of players and other bills being considered, *most bills are just noise* in the legislative process. A bill rises above the noise when other players care, and that is done by knowing and meeting the needs of those relatively few who can affect it. Be guided by the adage *self-interest is the engine of government.*

Politics trumps policy. Lawmakers and political parties vote their own best self-interests. The merits of any bill mean little relative to partisan party politics. To illustrate, for several years a Democratic senator was the lead sponsor for my principal's bill. The bill having moved through the House was now in the Senate and after years of lobbying we expected our bill to pass on "unanimous consent." However, that same year Republicans became the Senate majority. Republican leadership ordered that anything with our sponsor's name on it was "dead-on-arrival" without regard to the content of the legislation. Republican leadership did this because in two years, our Democratic sponsor would be up for re-election and they wanted to deny him a record of legislative achievement. He was a decent man and a good lawmaker and upon our request his staff released the bill to us to get a Republican sponsor. We got a Republican sponsor and our bill became law. Power is policy.

Follow the money. Money influences lawmakers in at least three ways: money into their campaign accounts; cash into their own personal pockets; and money into the state's treasury. Only extraordinary donation amounts receive any attention. At times money goes into lawmakers' pockets immediately by getting plum jobs and business opportunities; and later by getting well-paying lobbying jobs with friends they made while lawmakers.

Lawmakers are motivated by money they can keep in or direct into the state treasury. Lawmakers are also motivated by the promise of bringing more money into the treasury. For example, cash flow is a major enticement for states legalizing recreational marijuana. "States are addicted to cannabis tax revenues. According to a new report from New Frontier Data, [the few] states with legalized marijuana are on track to generate approximately $655 million in state taxes on retail sales in 2017. Within that tax figure, $559 million will come just from cannabis taxes, much more than from alcohol taxes."[192] Finally, by legalizing previously illegal behavior states save money on law enforcement, even when law enforcement itself opposes legalization for reasons of public safety.[193, 194]

Customers buy to meet their needs, not yours. Each lawmaker does his or her own cost-benefit calculation in deciding to support a bill.

"Lobbying is a dance of seduction." This means effective lobbyists present to lawmakers legislative opportunities so desirable lawmakers want to do what lobbyists suggest. In this sense, "seduction" means attraction to something positive.

"People don't like to be sold but they love to buy." Sales guru Geoffrey Gitomer says,

People buy things for emotional reasons and justify the reasons by using logic. I define it as the head being attached to the price, and the heart being attached to the wallet. If I pull on the heart-string, the wallet will pop out of the back pocket, and the only thing that can stop it is logic…The important thing to understand is that the old way of selling, which ties persuasiveness to techniques, is nowhere near as powerful as the person with the motive who wants to buy. And your biggest job in sales is to uncover the motive-or lose to someone who has.[195]

Emotions drive motives. Mr. Gitomer's point applied to lobbying means lawmakers' number one emotion is to protect their self-images and the public's perception of them. How well a product achieves that end is critical to making the sale.

SALES PACKAGES MUST BE CUSTOMIZED TO EACH LAWMAKER

Each legislator has personal motivators determining whether or not to purchase a legislative product. Were lobbying a *rational* process based on technical facts, and were public policy paramount, personal motivators would be less consequential. In reality, however, personal motivators are determinative.

A few among many possible motivators include: lawmaker self-interest; the desire for power, revenge, or both; keeping the backing of supporters, voters, and constituents; advice from legislative and agency staffs; demands of the party caucus; promotion of their personal politics; advancement of the public good; "doing the right thing;" and making the most of a bad situation.

The full meaning of the latter two motivators may not be so obvious. For example, "doing the right thing" may include a minority party lawmaker just trying to appear relevant. What constitutes doing the right thing is peculiar to each lawmaker. Making the most of a bad situation includes dealing with what seems to be inevitable, regardless of what the lawmaker wants. To illustrate, consider again recreational marijuana. A blue state Republican senator told me he opposes it. However, he feels that because his state first decriminalized marijuana, then legalized medical marijuana, that the next step of legalizing recreational marijuana is inevitable.[196] He reluctantly supports the recreational marijuana bill while attempting to incorporate into it a regulatory framework to reduce the overall mental health harm of marijuana consumption, especially upon adolescents.[197]

In our same conversation, a Democratic House member said he supports legalizing recreational marijuana so as not to miss out on tax revenues. He noted that since neighboring Northeastern states were enacting recreational marijuana laws; it is inevitable his state will do the same.[198] I perceived neither lawmaker actually wanted recreational marijuana, but seeing legalization as inevitable, they wanted to make the best of the situation.

SALES VENUES

Venues to influence lawmakers include in-person, in committee, the caucus, and through leadership. The most common and effective presentation is private and in-person and is the one upon which I focus. The other venues supplement but do not substitute for face-to-face, heart-to-heart meetings.

In-person. Advocacy is selling, not information transfer. Effective sales are face-to-face relations. Twitter, e-mail, instant messages, letters to the editor, social media, and advertisements all have their place in advocacy, but they *never* take the place of human interaction between advocate and a legislator or staff.

Legislators and staffs are smart and sophisticated; they know why advocates are there. They recognize lobbyists have a job to do just as they do. But if advocates come across as though they are visiting only to get something, rather than building relationships, they undermine their efforts. A relationship may later lead to making the sale, but it is built on a foundation of mutual respect and mutual benefit.

Other in-person venues. Other venues follow the face-to-face visits described above. Legislators can be approached in almost any public venue and in most, but not all, private or semiprivate settings. However, to illustrate an *inappropriate* venue, I was making this point to a *Lobby School* class when a recently retired lawmaker shouted, "No! No! No! I hated it when the doorbell would ring and I would answer in my robe to find a lobbyist at my front door handing me my morning newspaper!"

Lobbying in the district. There are times to lobby in a legislator's district and times not to, such as when the legislator is in the district to visit the home-folk. In states with full-time legislatures, lawmakers spend one-half to three-quarters of their time in the capital. They schedule district visits to meet with the people putting and keeping them in office, not with lobbyists. Intrusions on the lawmaker-constituent "family" time, may be considered an annoyance, and be counterproductive.

On the other hand, if a legislator is not in the district for the primary purpose of spending time with constituents, a visit could be welcome. He or she may be flattered having advocates traveling so far to visit.

Generally, the best time to lobby in the district is out of session and while not needing anything. During this non-needy moment, advocates cultivate relationships with the lawmaker on his or her home turf without the pressure of wanting his or her favorable action. An Iowa lawmaker advises, "Relationships in idle times pay big dividends in desperate times."

"Getting past nice." Unless a legislator has some animus toward the lobbyist or client, advocates can expect a pleasant visit. However, pleasantness isn't a vote. Being pleasant brings to the lawmaker a political benefit in the form of goodwill. Making a decision brings him or her political risk. Many legislators know how to be agreeable without making commitments. Lobbying is about securing votes, not just talking to lawmakers. Of course, advocates must be nice, but have to move beyond nice and reach the point where they say to the lawmaker or staffer, "Can we count on your vote?"

COMMITTEES AND COMMITTEE TESTIMONY

Committees. Normally, advocates close the sale just before a committee vote when they ask each lawmaker or staff, "Can I count on your vote?" If clients have the votes, they just need to show their face to the committee; if they definitely don't, they ask the sponsor to ask the chair not to take up the bill.

Over my career in the ten jurisdictions in which I worked to *move* legislation (as contrasted with stopping legislation), I have personally seen a committee only once negatively report a bill. Negative committee reports seldom happen because bill sponsors know recovering from a negative vote is extremely difficult. Therefore, the sponsor withdraws the bill. If a committee recommends the chamber *do not pass*, it isn't going to pass, but if the committee does not vote, at least there is a chance of taking the substance of the bill and amending it onto a germane bill moving forward.

However, in some instances, an advocate may decide to go ahead and gamble on the vote. This may occur if the client really needs a legislative fix this session, or has decided not to invest any more resources in the project, or the legislature is likely to be less amenable to the bill next year.

149

Once a bill has moved through committees of subject matter jurisdiction, it faces fiscal and procedural committees. Of special significance are the *calendar* and *conference* committees. The calendar committee, sometimes called Rules or other titles, schedules bills for floor consideration. Some calendar committees are ministerial, that is, they act like air traffic controllers making sure bills having passed through substantive committees are sent to the chamber floor in an orderly manner. Other calendar committees for reasons of politics may refuse to send targeted bills to the floor, thereby killing them.

A *conference committee* is created by the two chambers to resolve the chambers' differences over a bill. Each chamber appoints an equal number of *conferees*. In some states conference committees are rare or limited to budget matters. In other states almost all disputed bills are sent to conference committees. They may meet in secret to the consternation of the public and lobbyists.[199] A conference committee may rewrite entire bills or just resolve specific items in contention. The chambers' only choice is to accept or reject the *report of the conference committee* in an *up or down vote*, that is, no amendments. Conference committees can be so beyond the control of the two houses they have been called "the third house."[200]

Committee testimony. Committee testimony is a step in the process of passing a bill. A mid-Atlantic government affairs manager advises,

> Remember, though, that for major public policy issues the client must make a convincing case before the legislator or the agency if testifying in-person. A knowledgeable contract lobbyist should prepare the client for the demeanor of the committee (will it be late in the day, heavily dominated by members of one party, etc.), and will stress to the client the appropriate length that their presentation/testimony should be.[201]

Legislators are human beings who, like most of us, can be moved by stories touching their emotions. It helps when they look into the faces of people from their districts that would be greatly affected by a law. If a legislator is a member of a class of persons who would benefit from a proposal, he or she may be more inclined to support it. For example, if the legislator is a dog lover, and the law would help animal lovers in general, the legislator may be more attentive to a presentation. Lawmakers buy legislative products that make them feel good about themselves.[202]

CAUCUSES

Most lawmakers belong to one or more legislative caucuses, both party and topic. A legislative caucus is simply a grouping of legislators around a common interest. A caucus around a topic may be solution oriented rather than partisan. For example, a caucus may be interested in advancing agriculture and span party lines. However, the most important caucuses are party caucuses.

There are eighty-four party caucuses in the ninety-nine state legislative chambers. These are Democratic Party caucuses and Republican Party caucuses. Much of what happens in committee and on the chamber floor reflects what the majority caucus earlier decided to do. Most caucus decisions are made in private with only selected invitees; they are often—but now always—closed to the public, media, and of course the opposing party.

LEADERSHIP INFLUENCES COMMITTEE VOTES

I have seen repeated examples of leadership intervening on behalf of a bill so that lobbying anyone other than leadership became unnecessary. At times, leadership unexpectedly—at least *unexpectedly* to those not party to the deal—intervenes at the last moment to nullify months of lobbyists' work. To illustrate, a bill I had been working for months was about to be heard in subcommittee. The bill sponsor was present to testify. When the subcommittee chair called the bill up, its sponsor unexpectedly arose from the floor-level witness table and started handing out a revised version that neither subcommittee members, nor I, nor anyone else I knew had seen. The chair told the sponsor that at this meeting her subcommittee could not consider the revised bill since no one had seen it.

Following her statement, the sponsor walked over to stand face-to-face with her as she sat on the elevated dais. Just then the microphones were turned off. Suddenly the full committee chair entered the room by a side door and stood behind and above the subcommittee chair, literally "talking down" to the top of her head. I do not know what they said. After a few minutes, the full committee chair left the room, the sponsor returned to the witness table, the microphones were turned back on, and the subcommittee without discussion immediately and unanimously favorably reported the bill to the full committee. All it took was leadership unexpectedly intervening to move the bill. (I had no role in leadership "rolling" the subcommittee, although was I very happy with the result.)

DON'T RELY ON ONE-PARTY CONTROL OF THE LEGISLATURE

It would be a grave error to assume chamber control by a political party generally disposed to a bill would ensure favorable action by the legislature. Just because legislators are members of the same party doesn't mean they are all friends or work well together. They have supporters to satisfy, greater aspirations, political values, egos, and honest differences of opinion within their own caucus, chamber, and party. Chambers, even if run by the same party, can still fight with each other.

COMPASSION AND APPRECIATION FOR LAWMAKERS

Regardless of lawmakers' motives and personalities—"the good, the bad, and the ugly;" the idealist and the snollygoster; the smart and the not so smart; the egotist and the public servant; the part-timers and the full-timers—they share at least one thing in common: They put much time into being lawmakers. Briana Bierschbach writes that the time they put into lawmaking takes time away from other pursuits both professional and personal. And the time away from their livelihoods and their families takes a toll on them.[203] Beth-Ann Bloom in a comment to Ms. Bierschbach's article says,

> Legislators are expected to be in·multiple settings simultaneously. WE want to see them at parades, ribbon cuttings, and Moose Lodge meetings, but we also want them up-to-date on all sorts of state, local, and federal issues that require travel and meetings. WE want them to answer our calls, e-mails, and tweets, but we want them to interact with their colleagues and keep an eye on all the state agencies. WE want them to be effective which means seniority and being in the majority which requires fund-raising and campaigning not only for themselves but for their colleagues and newcomers. WE want them to meet with our mayor, school board, and town council as well as similar folks in the other cities in our district and we want them to be fine, up-standing family members, church-goers, and community volunteers.

> WE don't want to pay them, support them, or work with them, but we feel free to denigrate them and attack them if they leave office to work as lobbyists and consultants. Seems like WE are a big part of the problem. I hope WE are willing to change not just for the legislators' sake but for ours![204] (emphasis in original)

Lawmakers are attacked in the media and at home, their every action is scrutinized and criticized, privacy is forfeited, false friends surround them and at times their families, and party leadership regularly deprives them of making their own choices on how to vote and whom to support. They are targets for seduction and corruption by their own human weaknesses and manipulation by others.

And being in the minority party is even more thankless, especially if the legislature has changed party control. Those legislators' main choice is between quitting or staying irrelevant within the legislature they once ruled.[205] I've seen once-powerful lawmakers quit the legislature because being in the immaterial minority was too demeaning for former leaders.

Overall, lawmakers are decent people. While I've known a couple of arrogant, manipulative, full-of-themselves egotists, overwhelmingly the lawmakers with whom I worked were pleasant, civil, intelligent, and willing to listen—even to me a nonconstituent as long as what I offered benefitted them politically.

Lawmaking is a hard job for which legislators and staffs are due our appreciation. Friend or foe, they should be respected for the time and sacrifices they make. A *sincere* word or card of thanks is due them, and appreciation should be expressed liberally.

SUMMARY CHAPTER 11

While lawmakers are *politically* quaternary in importance, *constitutionally* they are primary since they are the only ones who vote to make a bill into statute. An advocate motivates legislators by knowing their political needs and how to satisfy them. Advocates should not be fooled if a legislator is "nice." The advocate's job is to move past nice to get the legislator's commitment. The Governor is the last step in getting your idea into statute which is the topic of the next chapter.

CHAPTER 12

LOBBYING THE GOVERNOR

The Governor, also called the Executive or Chief Executive, is the last *legislative* hurdle in a bill becoming a statute. All enrolled bills pass to him or her for approval or rejection.

The Constitution's *separation of powers* doctrine prohibits the legislative branch from implementing the laws it makes. The Founders predicted tyranny would result were either the legislative or executive branch authorized to both enact and implement laws.[206] Enactment of statutes belongs solely to the legislature. Implementation of statutes belongs solely to the executive, that is, the Governor.

The executive branch consists of the Governor and agencies that help him or her faithfully execute statutes. Going forward I use *administrative agency* and *executive agency* interchangeably.

Executive agencies decide whether or not a law ever goes into effect. Chapter 13, *Executive Agency Rulemaking, Appeal, and Enforcement*, discusses this but for now suffice to say: What the legislature *giveth*, an executive agency can *taketh* away; and what the legislature wouldn't give, an executive agency might.

ROLES OF THE GOVERNOR

With broad legal powers and thousands of employees, the Governor has profound authority and resources to carry out his or her roles.[207] The Governor's roles include:

Approving or disapproving enrolled bills. The Governor allows an enrolled bill to become a statute or vetoes it. From our perspective vetoes are our number one concern and are discussed below. However, in practice most Governors allow the vast majority of bills to become law.

Making and enforcing 90 percent of laws.[208] The Governor's agencies implement statutes by adopting and enforcing administrative rules; these rules are also laws. Of the body of law affecting a client, statutes make up about 10 percent and administrative rules make up 90 percent.

Issuing executive orders. The Governor's executive orders, also called *decrees*, instruct agencies how to administer a law. Since agencies work for the Governor and top agency managers are political appointees, either nominated or appointed by the Governor, agency implementation of the Governor's instructions is to be expected. Constitutionally, executive orders may not be appealable, administratively or judicially, if the agency possesses statutory authority to do as the Governor instructs.[209]

Affecting the legislature through veto and Governor-called special sessions. When the Governor vetoes an enrolled bill the legislature may reverse the veto either during or after the regular session. A post-regular session meeting of the legislature to reverse the governor's vetoes is called a *veto session*. Governors may also call *special sessions* to deal with limited topics. Legislatures are obligated to convene at the call of the Governor.

Budgeting and spending state money. The Governor proposes a budget to the legislature. The legislature revises the Governor's proposed budget into one or more bills which cover an *operating budget* to fund state agencies and a *capital budget* to buy and build things the Governor wants. The Governor's agencies administer hundreds of millions to several billions of state dollars.

Promoting general legislation. The Governor makes recommendations to the legislature for general laws, either detailed, bill-specific suggestions, or more general recommendations as in the Governor's annual *state of the state* message. In some states, the Governor's office is quite involved with general legislation while in other states it is not. If the legislature likes the Governor, it may pay attention, especially if the Governor is considered powerful and has good relationships with lawmakers. If the Governor and the legislature don't get along with each other they may continually battle. If the opposing party has a supermajority, it may simply ignore the Governor's budget requests and legislative suggestions.

However, the Governor can also ignore the legislature to some degree. That is, the Governor may attempt to direct the state via executive decrees. He or she may choose not to enforce the legislature's will as embodied in legislation. The Governor's agency can say, "We have no intention of enforcing this law and we will let the appropriation revert back to the general fund."

Commanding the National Guard. While the Governor's command of the National Guard is unlikely to affect most advocates, for completeness of our discussion, various Governors have considered the National Guard for staffing government in case of a state public employee union strike,[210] to fight drug trafficking,[211] and for border protection.[212]

The above are significant powers. However, it is the Governor's veto pen that may have the greatest impact for advocates.

VETOES

With some notable exceptions, such as New Mexico Governor Gary Johnson who claims to have vetoed 750 bills, most Governors veto few bills.[213] Governor Jerry Brown explained his small number of vetoes saying, "'There's a term called *comity*,' … 'It's a good old word, comity. It's the respect that one institution, or branch of government, owes to the other. And I follow that spirit.'"[214]

All 50 state Governors can veto whole legislative measures. In a large majority of states, a bill becomes law unless vetoed by the Governor within a specified number of days, the specific numbers varying among states.[215] In thirty-six states, Governors cannot edit budget riders.[216] For budget riders, it's veto everything or veto nothing.

In a smaller number of states, bills die unless formally signed by the Governor within a specified number of days. Not signing is called a *pocket veto* because the bill suffocates sitting in the Governor's pocket waiting for time to expire.

A *conditional veto* occurs when the Governor receives a bill to which he or she wants some changes and gives the legislature opportunity to change the bill to make it acceptable to him or her. If not changed, the bill will be fully vetoed. A Governor may also threaten, "I'm going to veto your enrolled bill unless you give me something or do something that I want."

In most states, Governors have the *line-item* veto to strike an appropriation from the budget. With a *reduction veto*, a Governor lowers a budget amount; with an *amendatory veto* the Governor revises legislation.

A *Frankenstein veto* occurs when a Governor vetoes individual words, thereby stitching together new legislation. Vetoing individual letters within words to rewrite legislation is known as a *Vanna White* veto.

Overriding a veto. A legislative "override" reverses a veto thereby moving the enrolled bill to law despite the Governor's objection. An override normally requires a supermajority vote of each chamber—normally two-thirds—or infrequently a bare majority.[217] If at least one-third of either chamber is of the Governor's party, and the Governor has a collegial relationship with his or her own party, the two-thirds vote will be very difficult to attain. However, when the Governor is fighting his or her own party, vetoes can be overridden even in a one party state.[218] For general bills, it may not be worth risking the Governor's political revenge for the legislature to override, even if they have the supermajority to do so.[219]

The Governor's veto may alienate the legislature which invested much effort in enrolling the bill. However, if the Governor's lobbyists function well, then lawmakers know beforehand of the likelihood of the veto and how to avoid it. Nevertheless, if the Governor has a poor working relationship with the legislature, a veto may seem to come from nowhere and further estrange the two branches of government.[220] The only thing rarer than a veto is a veto override.

PREDICTING A VETO AND VETO LETTER

A veto is always possible no matter how remote. While there are many reasons for a veto, the following may help predict one:

Agency objection. In the unlikely event that the legislature enrolls a bill over agency objections, when the legislature sends the enrolled bill to the Governor for approval, the agency may recommend a veto.

Separation of powers. If the Governor perceives the legislature is encroaching upon the executive branch, that is, creating a separation of powers violation, then expect a veto.

Impact on state budget. If a bill takes away money from the executive branch a veto is likely.[221] The Governor may veto a bill expecting the state would lose in expensive litigation.[222]

Tit-for-tat. When a legislature is not enrolling the Governor's bills, the Governor may say, in essence, "Since you lawmakers are refusing to enact the bills I or my agencies want, then I'm going to veto the bills you want."

Public outcry. Enough persons complaining, and especially threatening the economic viability of the state, may motivate the Governor to veto the work of the legislature.[223]

Governor's veto threats kill a bill. The Governor simply telling the legislature that a bill will be vetoed is often enough for the legislature to give up trying to enroll the bill. And all the more when leadership knows it doesn't have enough votes to override a veto.

Governor's policies. A former top gubernatorial aide advises,

> Sometimes, a Governor is philosophically or ideologically opposed—sometimes the Governor recognizes unintended consequences of similarly imposed laws in other states and at other times, new information reaches the Governor that gives him or her pause...If the Governor has expressed no public views, you can still take some cues from his or her prior policies, practices, or statements. Again your lobbyist can be extremely helpful on discerning the path forward.[224]

160

The veto letter. For bills that are important enough, the Governor may send a veto letter to the legislature. The letter explains to lawmakers what the Governor doesn't like about a bill and tells lawmakers what they need to do to meet the Governor's expectations. Some veto letters establish gubernatorial policy; forewarning lawmakers if they again send the Governor a bill with similar characteristics, that bill will also be vetoed.

In the theatre of politics, a Governor may express disapproval in more dramatic ways. For example, "The Democratic Governor [of West Virginia] publicly presented a tray of actual bull manure Thursday in the state capitol as he announced his veto of a Republican-backed budget package—leaving no doubt what he thinks of it."[225]

DON'T IGNORE THE GOVERNOR'S OFFICE

An advocate's level of involvement with the Governor's office depends on a number factors including:

1. Can the Governor influence special interests?

2. Can the Governor influence agencies?

3. How receptive will the Governor be to a specific bill?

4. Is there any chance of a veto?

5. Does the bill impact any of the Governor's bills?

6. Does the bill impact any agencies' bills?

7. Does the Governor's office lobby budget matters?

8. Does the Governor's office lobby general legislation? and

9. Does the legislature heed the Governor?

However, even with a Governor who vetoes few bills, advocates still need to run the traps with the Governor's office to make sure their bill is going to be approved by the Governor, either affirmatively or by default. Take nothing for granted. *To the degree appropriate,* clients and lobbyists should coordinate with the Governor's staff early in the process and then more closely as their bill appears headed for enactment.

Just as with the legislature, there is "no sure thing" with the Governor's office. To illustrate, the American Cancer Society's (ACS) former New Mexico lobbyist told me during a *Lobby School* class ACS asked New Mexico's First Lady Dee Johnson to be the point person for an ACS bill. She testified before the legislature and worked for the bill, and the legislature enacted the bill. Supporters of the bill thought they had a sure thing. However, her husband Governor Gary E. Johnson, who was known as "Dr. No" because of his high veto rate, vetoed the bill. Mrs. Johnson—according to the former ACS lobbyist—didn't speak to the Governor for weeks.

Governor's and agencies' lobbyists. The Governor's and the agencies' lobbyists, also called *legislative liaisons,* represent the executive branch before the legislature. As with all lobbyists, they draft legislation, negotiate with interested parties, line up witnesses, provide information, and testify before committees. Most importantly, legislative liaisons can become major legislative allies or opponents. In some states, they have to register as lobbyists, but, unlike nongovernment lobbyists, they may have access to the chamber floor during floor sessions.

Governor's staff. Governors rely on their staffs, as do most elected officials, so advocates must ensure staff is knowledgeable of their bills and their lobbying efforts. Support from the Governor's staff can move a bill to the Secretary of State to be codified; on the other hand, their opposition can send it bill back to the legislature with a veto message. A former top gubernatorial aide advises,

And don't forget the Governor's staff. When I was working as the Governor's communications director in Delaware, the Governor would occasionally informally ask my opinion about an issue ... typically, when we were in the car together. I knew he was looking for an unvarnished personal opinion stripped of the politics of people pro and con, and parties Republican or Democrat, and he knew I would tell him what I thought ... as a Delawarean.

Governors are human—they want their states to do well, and they want to leave good legacies in their steads. But many issues, some out of their immediate control, can trip up them or their staffs. The more information Governors and their staffs have, the better decisions they can make for the collective good of their states.[226]

The bill signing ceremony. Few things are more gratifying for advocates than participating in the Governor's signing of their bills into law. Most bill signing ceremonies are purely for fun and show; they generally have no legal significance. This is because strict constitutional timelines required the Governor to have approved a bill before there is time for a bill signing ceremony—typically several months. Once the session's bills are processed, the Governor has time for ceremonies.

In the theater of a bill signing ceremony, the Governor sits at his or her desk. Parties stand near the Governor while photographs are taken. The Governor may distribute favors such as pens emblazoned with the state seal and the Governor's signature.

SUMMARY CHAPTER 12

The Governor's office is the last step in a bill's journey and the fifth most important legislative influence in a bill becoming a statute. Governors permit most bills to become law. However, advocates must ensure their bill is not opposed by the governor or agencies in the legislature. They must be prepared to lobby in case of a potential veto.

A law does not exist until the relevant executive agency says it exists and tells you what it means. Agencies do this through the rulemaking process which I discuss in the final chapter.

CHAPTER 13

EXECUTIVE AGENCY RULEMAKING, APPEAL, AND ENFORCEMENT

What the legislature *giveth*, an executive agency can *taketh* away; and what the legislature wouldn't give, an executive agency might. Once enacted, the work of the legislature doesn't become *functioning* law until the appropriate agency makes it functioning law. In other words, a law doesn't exist until the agency says it exists; and no one knows what a law really means until the agency says what it means.

Although referring to the courts, Thomas Jefferson's comment, "The execution of laws is more important than the making of them,"[227] may be all the more true today when applied to executive agencies. This is because agencies possess legislative, executive, and judicial powers. They pass laws and send officers to enforce their laws. They prosecute and punish administratively and civilly for noncompliance with their laws. In an administrative proceeding, the agency itself is the lawgiver, accuser, witness, prosecutor, judge, jury, and executioner.

Agencies may act beyond the control of the Governor and legislature. University of California, Berkley Professor Clifford Dwight Waldo called the network of agencies the "administrative state" made up of a "governing class."[228] Herein I touch upon agency rulemaking, that is, the process by which an agency makes statutes into day-to-day reality— or not.

The Headless Fourth Branch of Government

Due to the perception that agencies are largely unaccountable, they have been called the "headless fourth branch of government."[229] While this description originally referred to independent federal executive agencies, today the *fourth branch of government* refers to government bureaucracy in general. Special interests fear agencies; legislators listen to agencies and don't generally contradict them; and Governors protect them. In this chapter we add another source of agency power: judges defer to them.

One may consider Federalist Number 10's concern that when legislative and administrative powers are united in the same body of magistrates the result is tyranny. With legislative, executive, and judicial powers, agencies have the opportunity for and sometimes do exercise a form of authoritarianism not envisioned by the Founders. Columbia University Constitutional Law scholar Phillip Hamburger states, "Administrative power thereby sidesteps most of the Constitution's procedural free-doms...Administrative power is thus all about the evasion of governance through law, including an evasion of constitutional processes and procedural rights."[230]

Agencies Regulate

Agencies exist to regulate. They often want *more* regulations because more regulations lead to more programs which lead to more employees and more power. And with greater numbers of programs, employees, and regulations, and the money that goes with them, the better the agency can carry out its mission, including implementing a statute.

However, regulation not efficiency is the goal of agencies. For example, they tend to be "program hoarders."[231] That is, agencies are loath to give up programs, whether needed or not. Discussing federal agencies, William Sanjour describes the bureaucratic perspective,

> So what's stopping us from doing it the right way? Almost everything. For starters the enforcement branches of the agency would lose a lot of personnel and authority and they wouldn't like that. Grades for supervisory civil servants are determined largely by the number and grades of people supervised, not by their effectiveness. Being more efficient with fewer people and a lower budget would mean a lot of demotions and lost jobs.[232]

He continues, "People who like to get things done, who need to see concrete results for their efforts, don't last long. They don't necessarily get fired, but they don't advance either; their responsibilities are transferred to others, and they often leave the agency in disgust."[233]

AGENCIES IMPLEMENT STATUTES THROUGH RULEMAKING

Agencies make statutes into day-to-day reality through making rules. As defined by the Federal Administrative Procedures Act (APA), "[Rule] means the whole or part of an agency statement of general or particular applicability and future effect designed to implement, interpret, or prescribe law or policy..."[234] Rulemaking is governed by procedural and substantive laws. The procedural is the "how" and the substantive is the "what." To have valid rules agencies must comport with both sets of requirements. Failure to abide by either is grounds for a court to nullify the rule.

Procedural governing law. The starting point for adopting and enforcing rules is the APA, state or federal. APAs were created to protect citizens from abuse of power by the *administrative state*.[235] Every action taken by an agency must comport with it. "Most states have adopted a body of statutes similar to the federal Administrative Procedures Act, or APA. These statutory schemes provide a series of rules that govern how an agency operates, how it promulgates rules, and how it must conduct administrative hearings and appeals."[236] In addition, many states base their APAs in whole or in part on the "State Administrative Procedure Act, Revised Model," published by the Uniform Law Commission.[237] While states' APAs intend to accomplish the same general goals, details differ somewhat among the states.

Substantive governing law. Substantive governing law, commonly called *enabling legislation*, is the statute(s) that specifically or inferentially enables an agency to adopt precise subject matter regulations. No agency rule is legal unless the agency can point to chapter and verse authority in the enabling legislation. A clearly written, detailed, well thought out statute keeps agency rulemaking within the bounds of the statute. However, if the statute is not clear and contains "ambiguities" then the agency has *to infer* in order to regulate. Professor Hamburger writes,

> [J]udges must defer to administrative interpretations of ambiguities in statutes. Such interpretations must be among the 'permissible' possible interpretations, but within this standard, agencies generally enjoy much freedom to choose their interpretations and thus to make law wherever they can find a plausible statutory ambiguity. As a result, even where Congress has not expressly authorized administrative rulemaking, agencies can use interpretations to make binding rules—that is, to make law.[238]

AGENCIES MAY "VETO" STATUTES

Agencies may negate statutes either by refusing to adopt rules or not enforcing the rules they adopt. Agency refusal to adopt or enforce rules for all practical purposes nullifies a law. Thomas Jefferson's, "The execution of laws is more important than the making of them," plays out when the agency says, "We have no intention of implementing this law and we are going to let the appropriation revert back to the general fund."

Upon adoption, the rule becomes final and enforceable. However, the agency may choose not to enforce it. "[A]n agency's decision not to prosecute or enforce ... is a decision generally committed to an agency's absolute discretion."[239] That is, agency non-enforcement may stand unless a court finds a rare case of agency "recalcitrance in the face of clear duty."[240] An agency makes a statute meaningless when it refuses to enforce the implementing rules, if any.

ADVOCATES NEED TO BE INVOLVED IN RULEMAKING

Advocates work with the agencies having jurisdiction over their laws to achieve three goals. First, defend their legislative win. The legislature gave them what they wanted, but that doesn't mean the agency is going to let them keep it. Second, to take away an opponent's legislative victory; an advocate may convince an agency to refuse to implement its opponent's legislation. Third, to get from the agency what the legislature didn't give. Lawmakers intentionally let interest groups during agency rulemaking fight out what the legislature couldn't or wouldn't deal with technically or politically. In rulemaking advocates may end up with more or with less.

ETHICS LAWS AND LOBBYIST REGISTRATION

Trying to influence an agency may be regulated as lobbying. Most statutory definitions of lobbying include legislative lobbying and executive lobbying in the same paragraph. However, a state may have separate laws for legislative and agency lobbying. States may also have different regulatory bodies and rules for legislative and agency lobbyists. Many states publish manuals to guide lobbyists in compliance with agency statutory and administrative lobbying requirements. Advocates must at a minimum register and report their expenditures when lobbying an agency.

RULEMAKING PROCESS

Since an agency's purpose is to regulate, advocates should approach the agency with the presumption the agency is going to promulgate rules to implement their law. While the APA provides for public input into rulemaking, the agency may or may not want to hear it.

The rule may be final before anyone sees it. Sometimes for *all practical purposes* a proposed rule is final before the public sees it. This is because the agency invested months or even years in writing the draft rule, it completed negotiations with interested parties, and it has no intention of "going back to the drawing board" to change the proposed rule. The agency has too many other new rules to write.

Agency unwillingness to change substantive portions of a draft rule makes the formal adoption hearing *pro forma*. To illustrate, I participated in a state rulemaking during which agency staff conducting the hearing were constantly looking at their watches and yawning. Finally, the chief agency officer looked up and said, "Could industry please hurry this thing up? You see we've already decided what we are going to do, but the APA says we have to listen to you. So please hurry it up."

However, despite the above illustration and while core provisions of the rule are most likely "a done deal," an agency may yet consider minor changes. If advocates can help an agency achieve a better version of its rule without sending the agency back to the drawing boards, the agency may revise the proposed rule at least on the margins.

Normal rulemaking process. Normally, rulemaking is an open process to which the public has full access as governed by the APA. Of interest to us in this chapter is the APA requirement that executive agencies inform citizens about proposed agency rulemaking affecting their substantial interests and for agencies to provide opportunity for public input and appeal.

Professor Cornelius M. Kerwin writes as to development of the original federal APA,

> The core elements of rulemaking as put forward in the Administrative Procedure Act can be expressed in three words: information, participation, and accountability. These are familiar principles basic to our constitutional democracy. In the context of rulemaking, however, they assume forms and meanings different from those in other political settings.

> The most basic element of 'information' in rulemaking is the notice provided to the public at large when a rule is being developed and when it becomes final and binding...Another is implied in the statement of basis and purpose. That is the information the agencies rely on to develop the rule...

> The agencies were obliged to allow written comments but participation in any other form was not a matter of right. Surprisingly, the agencies were not instructed anywhere in the act to take heed of what they learned from the public in written comments or in whatever other form of participation they allowed...

> The primary vehicle for accountability in the APA was judicial review. As outlined in section 706 of the act, judicial review is paradoxical. On the one hand the act made the courts available to those who wished to challenge rules...On the other hand the standard against which agencies' rulemaking decisions would be

judged was anything but strict. Rulemaking could be judged on both substantive and procedural dimensions but in neither were agencies given difficult criteria to meet . . . [241]

Professor Kerwin goes on to explain while the APA has not changed, implementation and practice have. However, "A grasp of the APA's original provisions is an important foundation for understanding current process, nevertheless."[242]

OVERCOMING A FINAL RULE

Successfully challenging, negating, or otherwise overcoming an agency's *final* regulation is extremely difficult, if not impossible. To reverse a rule I recommend following this sequence of appeal, which I gradate based upon incrementing costs in time and money: administrative appeal which includes the agency itself, the Governor, or administrative hearing; legislative appeal; and finally judicial appeal.

Administrative appeal. Petition the agency to enter into rulemaking to reverse the objectionable portions of the rule. With good lobbying and luck, the agency could decide to reconsider a rule or decision.

Next, ask the Governor to intervene with the agency. Nominally, an agency works for the Governor. If the agency is politically aligned with the Governor, it may be willing to reconsider the rule to coincide with the Governor's wishes. On the other hand, agency staff may do pretty much what it wants without regard to the Governor.

Finally, challenge agency action in an administrative proceeding. In contrast with a judicial forum, an administrative hearing aims at communicating fairness and civility. However, a state administrative hearing officer told me plaintiffs almost always lose before him because the whole process is so "stacked against them" and in favor of the agency.

A federal agency general counsel told me his agency wins 90 percent of its cases. And the best a hearing officer may do is to make a *recommendation* to the agency which it may or may not accept.

Legislative appeal. The legislature can repeal or revise the enabling legislation or defund the agency's enforcement of the rule. It can adopt a highly detailed statute with few ambiguities thereby reducing regulatory "holes" to fill and limiting agency regulatory discretion. The legislature can draft appropriations and riders that are so specific agencies risk somewhat reduced funding if they fail to carry out legislative directions.

In many states, agency rules may not go into effect until approved by the legislature. The agency may be motivated to give advocates what they want fearing advocates might have enough influence with the legislature to convince it to deny the agency something it wants, such as funding, staffing, or authority. Clients and lobbyists may make some lifelong enemies within an agency by going to the legislature, but if that's what they need to do and it's worth the price, go ahead and try it.

Judicial appeal. Advocates can attempt a judicial appeal. However, they should expect to pay high transactional costs and still lose because agencies as a *matter of law* are presumed to act legally. The presumption is rebuttable but petitioners face a steep legal climb to challenge it successfully. Professor Hamburger as to judicial review writes, "When the government is party to a case, the doctrines that require judicial deference to agency interpretation are precommitments in favor of the government's legal position, and the effect is systematic judicial bias [i.e., in favor of the government]."[243] Further, agency decisions generally only have to be supported by *substantial evidence* which means evidence weighing more than a scintilla. As the hearing officer stated above, it's all stacked against the plaintiff and in the favor of government.

AGENCY STAFFS

Agency staffs consist of two groups: career civil service and political appointees. While both are critical to implementing a law, each entity thinks quite differently from the other.

Career civil service. Career civil service staffs make up the bulk of agency personnel. They work for governmental agencies to serve their communities and agencies' ideals. For example, early in my career as an idealistic agency enforcement officer my motive was protection of the environment. Similar idealism is common among agency staff.

Civil service employees by law are generally insulated from political control that could impede them from carrying out the mission of the agency and implementation of the legislature's instructions. However, these same job protections may shield employees and their agencies from accountability to the legislature, the Governor, and the courts.[244]

Political appointees. Political appointees are an agency's top management put there to carry out the Governor's agenda. However, ability to direct the agency is limited because their constitutional duty is to *faithfully execute* the legislature's instructions and because civil service employees, absent high crimes and treason, cannot be fired and barely can be disciplined for undermining political appointees.

Political appointees attempting to direct civil service staff may risk legislative wrath and media "bad press." Bad press especially undermines the reputation of the agency with the public. And it upsets the Governor, who generally wants state agencies to do their jobs quietly and without distracting the Governor and political appointees from their own priorities. The Governor doesn't have the time, staff, political capital, or interest to become involved in the operations of most agencies. Political appointees are intimidated by fears of agency employee whistleblowing, whether the claims are true or not.

Political appointees, at least nominally, serve the Governor. They will think how the Governor thinks and do what he or she wants. An advocate's *positive* relationship with the Governor's office should help it influence an agency. However, advocates having a difficult relationship with the Governor's office can expect to have a similarly difficult time working with the agency's political appointees. And neither civil service employees nor political appointees want parties outside the agency interfering with agency wishes or telling them what to do.

Even after the agency promulgates rules to implement a law, it may come to nothing if the agency doesn't enforce its rules. Enforcement is especially important when agencies use it to go after their enemies.

AGENCY ENFORCEMENT

Agencies may formally and informally enforce their rules. Formal enforcement starts with monitoring regulated parties' reports or operations or site inspection. Formal penalties include fines, loss of permits to operate, suspensions or revocations of professional licenses, and, in the case of criminal prosecution, imprisonment.

Informal enforcement can include more frequent inspections or other scrutiny of a regulated party. Sometimes the threat of being subjected to a heightened level of agency scrutiny, however informal and resembling harassment, may convince a regulated party to conform more closely to and cooperate with agency expectations and enforcement personnel.

Government in general knows that *the process is the punishment*.[245] To illustrate, a state lobbyist for an organization having lobbyists in 46 states told his *Lobby School* class that his affiliate sued a state agency. He said while their lawyers won every step in the process, in the end they had to drop their challenge because the agency drained them financially through discovery, depositions, motion hearings, and the like. Few private organizations, even a substantial one such as his, have funds sufficient to match the resources of a state agency dedicated to spending state money to overwhelm an opponent. When dealing with agencies, *the process is the punishment.* And they know it.

BEST LOBBYISTS FOR AGENCIES

Agency staffs tend to be well educated. Public employees, for example, have three times the rate of advanced degrees as those working in the private sector.[246] In addition, regulation-heavy states pay high wages and benefits to attract and keep them. This means that an agency lobbyist must be able to understand and contribute to complex technical arguments with educated and experienced professionals.

Agency lobbyists should intimately understand the enabling legislation and legal context in which rulemaking fits. He or she must know the minutia of the proposed rule and be able to make useful, line-by-line, word-by-word, and calculation-by-calculation technical suggestions about the proposed rule. The lobbyist also must intimately know the state APA or have colleagues who do. A lobbyist having worked for an agency or having an advanced technical degree and appropriate professional credentials, such as licenses and publications, has greater influence with agency technical staff and is of greater value during the rulemaking process.

The need for an agency lobbyist to be in the state capital for rulemaking is convenient but not critical. Agency rulemaking and public hearing venues may be situated all over the state and, unlike lobbying the legislature, much agency "facts and law" lobbying can be done remotely.

SUMMARY CHAPTER 13

Executive agencies establish administrative laws that determine how a statute is to be implemented. Once agency staff has written and published the proposed rules, it is usually too late to do much about them. Once rules are final amending or reversing them is extremely difficult, if not impossible.

Agency lobbying is deliberative, fact-based, and very technical. An agency lobbyist should have the academic credentials and experience enabling him or her to work with agency experts and earn their respect.

BEST WISHES

Dear Reader, I hope this book accomplishes for you the purpose for which it was written: to help you understand better lawmaking's practices, pressures and foibles, lusts and noble moments; give insights into players' souls and driving forces; and make more human and comprehensible the process of making laws. Please let me know your thoughts about this work, comments, and suggestions to improve the book for future readers.

At *www.insiderstalkwinning.com* you can find information about our other books, on-line advocacy skills training, live legislative and agency lobbying seminars, and presentations customized for your needs and delivered at your location.

ABOUT THE AUTHOR

Robert Guyer lobbied at the state, federal, and international levels both as an in-house and contract lobbyist. He is a graduate of the University of Florida holding degrees in political science, civil engineering, and law; and is admitted to the practice of law in Florida and the District of Columbia. You may learn more about him, his *Lobby School*, and effective advocacy techniques at www.lobbyschool.com. You may contact him at *rlguyer@lobbyschool.com* or through the website *www.insiderstalkwinning.com*.

ENDNOTES

1 John L. Zorack, *The Lobbying Handbook* (Washington, D.C.: Professional Lobbying and Consulting Center, 1990), 773.

2 A bill is "enrolled" when the political and administrative leaders of each chamber certify it has been approved by their chambers. An enrolled bill goes to the executive, President at the Federal level or Governor at the state level, for executive action, approval, or veto.

3 Campaign manager, e-mail communication with author, March 7, 2017.

4 Media consultant, LinkedIn communication with author, 2014.

5 Association lobbyist, e-mail communication with author, November 2, 2017.

6 President, managed health care system, e-mail communication with author, October 31, 2017.

7 "A short official note, typically recording a sum owed." *English Oxford Living Dictionaries* accessed August 28, 2017, https://en.oxforddictionaries.com/definition/chit.

8   Sen. Uvalde Lindsey (D, Fayetteville, AR), personal conversation with author, December 18, 2014.

9   Florida Senator, presentation to Florida Chemical and Manufacturers Council, circa 1995.

10 Nebraska only has one chamber, a senate, making 99 total U.S. chambers.

11 "The Federalist Number 10: The Utility of the Union as a Safeguard Against Domestic Faction and Insurrection (continued)," *Constitution Society*, last modified May 30, 2017, http://www.constitution.org/fed/federa10.htm.

12 *The Lobbying Handbook*, 679.

13 "A short official note, typically recording a sum owed." *English Oxford Living Dictionaries* accessed August 28, 2017, https://en.oxforddictionaries.com/definition/chit.

14 *The Lobbying Handbook*, 732.

15 Robert Guyer and Dean Griffith, "Succeeding in the State Legislature," *PT: Magazine of Physical Therapy*, 9, no. 3 (2001), 46.

16 Alex Blumberg, "Forget Stocks or Bonds, Invest in a Lobbyist," *National Public Radio: Planet Money*, January 6, 2012, http://www.npr.org/sections/money/2012/01/06/144737864/forget-stocks-or-bonds-invest-in-a-lobbyist.

17 Donald deKieffer, *The Citizen's Guide to Lobbying Congress* (Chicago: Chicago Review Press, 1997), 168.

18 Government affairs manager, e-mail communication with author, August 2, 2017.

19 "Succeeding in the State Legislature," 46.

20 Jeffrey H. Birnbaum, *The Lobbyists* (New York: Random House, 1993), 198.

21 Mark Foley, "Re: Guide to Lobbyists and Lobbying," e-mail communication with author, February 27, 2016.

22 Senate Speaker Ramsey said this to a meeting of the Tennessee Lobbyists Association, circa 2009.

23 Nilofer Merchant, "Culture Trumps Strategy Every Time," *Harvard Business Review*, March 2, 2011, https://hbr.org/2011/03/culture-trumps-strategy-every.

24 "Lobbying in Rhode Island," *Rhode Island Department of State*, 2017, accessed November 12, 2017, http://www.sos.ri.gov/divisions/open-government/transparency/lobbying/lobbying-hotline-form.

25 Doug Mann of Littlejohn and Mann, Tallahassee, Florida said this during his 2002 guest lecture to my graduate class at Florida State University where I served as a visiting professor.

26 Alan Rosenthal, *The Third House: Lobbyists and Lobbying in the States* (Washington, D.C.: CQ Press, 2001), 241.

27 Government affairs manager, e-mail communication with author, November 26, 2015.

28 *The Lobbying Handbook*, 692.

29 Robert Wechsler, *The Regulation of Local Lobbying*, (North Haven, CT: City Ethics Inc., 2016), accessed January 29, 2018, http://www.cityethics.org/files/Regulation-of-Local-Lobbying-Robert-Wechsler.pdf, 6.

30 Craig Holman, Ph.D. and Thomas Susman, Esq., "Self-Regulation and Regulation of the Lobbying Profession," *OECD: Global Forum on Public Governance*, April 23, 2009, http://www.citizen.org/documents/Self-Regulation-and-Regulation-of-Lobbying.pdf, 6.

31 *The Lobbyists*, 190.

[32] Government affairs manager, e-mail communication with author, July 20, 2014.

[33] Winston Churchill, *Brainy Quotes*, accessed July 27, 2017, https://www.brainyquote.com/quotes/quotes/w/winstonchu136788.html.

[34] California contract lobbyist, LinkedIn communication with author, October 4, 2017.

[35] Rebecca Beitsch, "Stalled Progress for Women in State Legislatures," *The Pew Charitable Trusts: Stateline*, December 8, 2015, http://www.pewtrusts.org/en/research-and-analysis/blogs/stateline/2015/12/08/stalled-progress-for-women-in-state-legislatures.

[36] Karl Kurtz, "Who We Elect: The Demographics of State Legislatures," *NCSL: State Legislatures Magazine*, December 1, 2015, http://www.ncsl.org/research/about-state-legislatures/who-we-elect.aspx.

[37] Barron Young Smith, "Why Do So Many Politicians Have Daddy Issues?," *Slate*, August 22, 2012, http://www.slate.com/authors.barron_youngsmith.html.

[38] David Brooks, "All Politics Is Thymotic," *The New York Times*, March 19, 2006, http://query.nytimes.com/gst/fullpage.html?res=9A01EFD81E31F93AA25750C0A9609C8B63.

[39] Alice Walton, "Villaraigosa: Politicians 'Want To Be Loved and Want To Be Popular,'" *Radio station 89.3 KPCC*, July 20, 2012, http://www.scpr.org/blogs/news/2012/07/20/9079/villaraigosa-politicians-want-be-loved-and-want-be/.

[40] Matthew Larotonda, "New Jersey Governor Chris Christie 'Not Looking to Be Loved,'" *ABC News: Good Morning America*, May 5, 2012, http://abcnews.go.com/blogs/politics/2012/05/new-jersey-Governor-chris-christie-not-looking-to-be-loved/.

41   Malcom Andrew, "*Oh-oh!* Politicians Share Personality
      Traits with Serial Killers: Study," *Los Angeles Times*,
      June 15, 2009, http://latimesblogs.latimes.com/
      washington/2009/06/politicians-and-serial-killers.html.

42   Leadership Institute's *Campaign Management School*, June
      2014. Sutton has managed numerous political campaigns from
      city council to U.S. Congress. https://www.leadershipinstitute.
      org/contactus/staff.cfm?staff=950 for information on him.

43   *Campaign Management School*, June 2014.

44   *Campaign Management School*, June 2014.

45   Cheryl Boudreau, "The Persuasion Effects of Political
      Endorsements," Center for the Study of Democracy,
      accessed March 27, 2018, www.democracy.uci.edu.

46   Aaron Marshall, "Despite Laws Against Lying, Tall
      Tales Have Become the Norm on the Campaign
      Trail, Experts Say," *The Cleveland Plain Dealer*, October
      29, 2012, http://www.cleveland.com/open/index.
      ssf/2012/10/despite_laws_against_lying_tal.html.

47   "Despite Laws Against Lying."

48   Peter Sage, "Politics 101. It's the turnout stupid," *Up Close
      with Peter Sage*, August 29, 2017, peterwsage.blogspot.com.

49   "One, especially a politician, who is guided by personal advantage
      rather than by consistent, respectable principles." "Snollygoster,"
      Your Dictionary, accessed January 16, 2018, http://www.
      yourdictionary.com/snollygoster#HLFhdukpDOzWUDcT.99.

50   Lord Acton (John Emerich Edward Dalberg) Letter to
      Archbishop Mandell Creighton, April 5, 1887, *Hanover
      College History Department*, accessed January 16, 2018, https://
      history.hanover.edu/courses/excerpts/165acton.html.

51 Kenneth Ashworth, *Caught Between the Dog and the Fireplug, Or How to Survive Public Service* (Washington, D.C. : Georgetown University Press, 2001), 17.

52 Political consultant, e-mail communication with author, February 24, 2017.

53 "Illinois has the wrong legislature: Too many risk-averse pols," *Chicago Tribune*, February 12, 2017, http://www.chicagotribune. com/news/opinion/editorials/ct-illinois-budget-cullerton-radogno-rauner-madigan-edit-0212-20170210-story.html.

54 "5 Democrats to Watch," *Time 2016*, accessed January 16, 2018, http://content.time.com/time/specials/packages/article/0,28804,1834724_1834723_1834714,00.html.

55 Sid Rich, *The Lobbyist: An Insider's Look at the Legislative Process* (Frederick, MD: America Star Books, 2010), 11.

56 Kevin Derby, "Daphne Campbell Demands Apology from Fellow House Dems," *Sunshine State News*, May 1, 2011, http://www.sunshinestatenews.com/story/daphne-campbell-demands-apology-fellow-House-dems.

57 "Florida 2014 Legislative Scorecard," *Liberty First Network*, accessed January 11, 2018, https://www.scribd.com/document/227670153/2014-LFN-Florida-Legislative-Scorecard.

58 "The exchange of support or favors, especially by legislators for mutual political gain by voting for each other's bills." "Logrolling,"*Dictionary.com*, accessed July 31, 2017, http://www.dictionary.com/browse/logrolling.

59 Lawmaker, personal communication with author, circa 1994.

60 Bob Dole, *Great Presidential Wit* (New York: Simon and Shuster, 2001), 220.

61 Steve Straub, "Benjamin Franklin Poster, Would you persuade, speak of Interest, not of Reason," *The Federalist*

Papers Project, August 6, 2012, http://thefederalistpapers.
org/posters/benjamin-franklin/benjamin-franklin-poster-
would-you-persuade-speak-of-interest-not-of-reason.

62 I first heard "facts don't vote" from Florida House
staff Ron Phillips who at the time also was a graduate
student in the lobbying class I taught at Florida State
University. As of this writing Ron is President and CEO
of Republic Consultants, LLC, and of-counsel to Gavel
Resources, both Washington, D.C. lobbying firms.

63 *The Lobbying Handbook*, 692.

64 Bradford Fitch, *Citizen's Handbook to Influencing Elected
Officials: Citizen Advocacy in State Legislatures and
Congress* (Alexandria, VA: CapitolNet, 2010), 48.

65 Ron Haskins and Greg Margolis, *Show Me the Evidence*.
(Washington, D.C.: Brookings Institution Press, 2014).
Cited in E. J. Dionne, "In Politics Does Evidence Matter?,"
The Washington Post, December 7, 2014, https://www.
washingtonpost.com/opinions/ej-dionne-in-politics-does-
evidence-matter/2014/12/07/a819969c-7ca3-11e4-b821-
503cc7efed9e_story.html?utm_term=.d1c878299458.

66 Contract lobbyist, e-mail communication with author, June 2017.

67 "Thomas Jefferson Quotes," *BrainyQuote*, accessed
January 16, 2018, https://www.brainyquote.com/
quotes/quotes/t/thomasjeff107328.html.

68 Brian Resnik, "How Power Corrupts the Mind: Pity the Despot,"
The Atlantic, July 9, 2013, http://www.theatlantic.com/health/
archive/2013/07/how-power-corrupts-the-mind/277638/.

69 "Edmund Burke Quotes," *WinWisdom Quotations*,
accessed January 16, 2018, http://www.winwisdom.
com/quotes/author/edmund-burke.aspx.

70 Nicholas Kusnetz, "Secrecy, corruption and conflicts of interest pervade state governments," *USA Today*, November 9, 2015, https://www.usatoday.com/story/news/2015/11/09/center-integrity-corruption-grades-states/74823212/.

71 Beth Rucker, "Ethics Reforms Didn't Take Away Lobbyists' Power, Bredesen Says," *The Daily News*, July 31, 2007, https://www.memphisdailynews.com/news/2007/jul/31/ethics-reforms-didnt-take-away-lobbyists-power-bredesen-says/.

72 Stephen Sherrill, "The Year in Ideas: A to Z.; Acquired Situational Narcissism," *The New York Times Magazine*, December 9, 2001, http://www.nytimes.com/2001/12/09/magazine/the-year-in-ideas-a-to-z-acquired-situational-narcissism.html.

73 Adam Grant, "Yes, Power Corrupts, But Power Also Reveals," *Psychology Today*, April 21, 2013, https://www.psychologytoday.com/blog/give-and-take/201304/yes-power-corrupts-power-also-reveals.

74 "Yes, Power Corrupts, But Power Also Reveals."

75 Katherine A. DeCelles, et al., "Does Power Corrupt or Enable? When and Why Power Facilitates Self-Interested Behavior," and the quote—*which appears in an abstract*—can be found at National Institute of Health; National Center for Biotechnology Information, U.S. National Library of Medicine, *Abstract PubMed*, January 16, 2012, https://www.ncbi.nlm.nih.gov/pubmed/22250668.

76 *The Quotations Page*, accessed January 18, 2018, http://www.quotationspage.com/quote/29416.html.

77 Howard Blume, Victoria Kim, and James Rainey, "FBI Seizes LAUSD Records Related to Troubled iPad Program," *Los Angeles Times*, December 2, 2014, http://www.latimes.com/local/education/la-me-lausd-ipads-20141203-story.html.

78 Robert Barnes, "Supreme Court overturns corruption conviction of former Va. Governor McDonnell," *The Washington Post*, June 27, 2016, https://www.washingtonpost.com/politics/supreme-court-rules-unanimously-in-favor-of-former-va-robert-f-mcdonnell-in-corruption-case/2016/06/27/38526a94-3c75-11e6-a66f-aa6c1883b6b1_story.html?utm_term=.6543ada4a75a.

79 Grace Wyler and Zeke Miller, "BEYOND INSIDER TRADING: Here's How Members Of Congress Get Rich Off Earmarks," *Business Insider*, November 15, 2011, http://www.businessinsider.com/congress-insider-trading-earmarks-real-estate-nancy-pelosi-rich-tax-payer-money-2011-11.

80 Nicholas Kusnetz, "Conflicts of interest run rampant in state legislatures," *The Center for Public Integrity*, May 19, 2014, https://www.publicintegrity.org/2013/03/18/12313/conflicts-interest-run-rampant-state-legislatures.

81 Eric Eyre, "After Frontier dismissal, WV Senate head hired by rival Citynet," *Charleston Gazette Mail*, September 5, 2017, https://www.wvgazettemail.com/news/after-frontier-dismissal-wv-Senate-head-hired-by-rival-citynet/article_923b29e6-9a0d-5b6d-b0b0-0d551278190b.html.

82 Jay Michael and Dan Walters with Dan Weintraub, *The Third House: Lobbyists, Money, and Power in Sacramento* (Berkeley, CA: Berkeley Public Policy Press, 2002), 89.

83 Tal Kopan, "Report Finds Michigan Lawmakers in Scandal Abused Office," *CNN*, September 1, 2015, http://www.cnn.com/2015/09/01/politics/todd-courser-cindy-gamrat-wrongdoing-report/.

84 "Jack Abramoff: The Lobbyist's Playbook," *CBS News 60 Minutes*, November 6, 2011, https://www.youtube.com/watch?v=CHiicN0Kg10.

85   Ian H. Robertson, "Petraeus, Sex and the Aphrodisiac of Power," *Psychology Today*, November 13, 2012, https://www. psychologytoday.com/blog/the-winner-effect/201211/ petraeus-sex-and-the-aphrodisiac-power-0.

86   Younger female *Lobby School* participants never have shared receiving unwanted sexual advances from lawmakers. While I have no data as to why mature women do and young woman don't, possible reasons may include: they haven't been in the legislature long enough, lawmakers pursue age-appropriate relationships, or they are too shy to mention them.

87   Dr. John Ng, "Why Nice Women Are Attracted to Powerful Men," *Leadership.com.sg*, May 24, 2016, http:// www.leadership.com.sg/blog/why-nice-women-are-attracted-to-powerful-men/#.WX9-FYTyuUk.

88   Henry Kissinger, *Quote Db*, accessed July 31, 2017, https://www.quotedb.com/quotes/1467.

89   Marcus Baram, "Power, Influence and Sex Appeal," *ABCNews*, February 22, 2008, http://abcnews. go.com/Politics/story?id=4331455&page=1.

90   A mature female reviewer of this book writes, "This anecdote, while undoubtedly an accurate appraisal of that person's views, may offend some readers given that it depicts an offensive *quid pro quo* ('grab your butt') where toleration is the price one pays for success. Some individuals might see these paragraphs as hinting that one should hire a lobbyist who can put up with sexual advances as a means of moving legislation. (Please consider also the potential that male readers will see women that they may encounter in the capitol not as competitors but as prostitutes—whether warranted or not—where the process of legislation is concerned.)"

91   Julie Vojtech, e-mail communication to author, July 20, 2014.

92 Jay Michael and Dan Walter, *The Third House*, 81.

93 "Law Maker Resigns after Sex Comments Are Broadcast," *Sky Valley Chronicle*, September 10, 2009, http://www. skyvalleychronicle.com/Breaking-News/Law-Maker-Resigns-After-Sex-Comments-Are-Broadcast-164405.

94 David Mortosko, "'Obama 'sucked less than Romney': Former Sen. Bob Kerrey, a DEMOCRAT, uncorks a Nebraska-sized tornado on the president, slamming him for health care lies and saying he's not up to saving Social Security," *Daily Mail.com*, March 28, 2014, http://www. dailymail.co.uk/news/article-2591304/Obama-sucked-Romney-Former-Sen-Bob-Kerrey-DEMOCRAT-uncorks-Nebraska-sized-tornado-president-slamming-Obamacare-lies-saying-hes-not-saving-Social-Security.html.

95 Dana Carney, "Defend Your Research: Powerful People Are Better Liars," *Harvard Business Review*, May, 2010, https://hbr.org/2010/05/defend-your-research-powerful-people-are-better-liars.

96 "Alabama Legislators, Staff Member, Lobbyists and Businessmen Charged in 39-count Indictment for Roles in Wide-ranging Conspiracy to Influence and Corrupt Votes Related to Electronic Bingo Legislation," *U.S. Department of Justice, Office of Public Affairs*, October 4, 2010, https://www. justice.gov/opa/pr/alabama-legislators-staff-member-lobbyists-and-businessmen-charged-39-count-indictment-roles.

97 Sean Collins Walsh, "Ex-aide: Rep. Dawnna Dukes billed state for days she wasn't at Capitol," *American-Statesman*, May 19, 2016, http://www.statesman. com/news/state--regional-govt--politics/aide-rep-dawnna-dukes-billed-state-for-days-she-wasn-capitol/TU7xkk5jWdia7U3ARIMz9I/.

98 Lisa Robinson, "Former aide to Catherine Pugh indicted on election law violations," *WBALTV*, January 9, 2017, http://www.wbaltv.com/article/former-aide-to-catherine-pugh-indicted-on-election-law-violations/8577996.

99 "Eachus Staff Member Among 12 Indicted In Misuse Of State Money Scandal," *Times Leader*, June 22, 2015, http://timesleader.com/archive/271334/stories-eachus-staff-member-among-12-indicted-in-misuse-of-state-money-scandal114989.

100 Gilad Edelman, "Former Legislative Aide Pleads Guilty to Misdemeanors," *The Texas Tribune*, June 17, 2014, https://www.texastribune.org/2014/06/17/former-legislative-aide-pleads-guilty-misdemeanors/.

101 Jay Michael and Dan Walters, *The Third House*, 30.

102 Jason Hancock, "Missouri legislative staffers earn big money as political consultants," *Kansas City Star*, December 20, 2015, http://www.kansascity.com/news/politics-government/article50828510.html.

103 Madison Park, MJ Lee, and Rebecca Berg, "Missouri Gov. Eric Greitens admits to affair but denies blackmail allegation," *CNN*, January 11, 2018, http://www.cnn.com/2018/01/11/politics/eric-greitens-affair/index.html.

104 Erika Holst, "Illinois Governors in trouble," *Illinois Times*, February 26, 2015, http://illinoistimes.com/article-15149-illinois-Governors-in-trouble.html.

105 Thomas J. Gradel and Dick Simpson, *Corrupt Illinois: Patronage, Cronyism, and Criminality*, (Urbana: University of Illinois Press, January 20, 2015), Kindle Edition.

106 "Former Alabama Governor Don Siegelman Re-Sentenced on Bribery, Conspiracy, Fraud and Obstruction of Justice Charges," *U.S. Department of Justice, Office of*

Public Affairs, August 3, 2012, https://www.justice.gov/opa/pr/former-alabama-Governor-don-siegelman-re-sentenced-bribery-conspiracy-fraud-and-obstruction.

107 Jared Brey, "John Estey, Rendell's Former Chief-of-Staff, Charged With Wire Fraud," *Philadelphia Magazine,* April 29, 2016, http://www.phillymag.com/news/2016/04/29/ed-rendell-john-estey-wire-fraud/#XY47XtWbk3JW4TEw.99.

108 Abbott Koloff, "Federal prosecutors say Christie aides lied about GWB closures," *NorthJersey.com,* March 11, 2016, http://www.northjersey.com/story/news/2016/03/11/federal-prosecutors-say-christie-aides-lied-about-gwb-closures/94543670/.

109 Priscilla DeGregory and Bruce Golding, "Ex-Cuomo aide convicted on corruption charges," *New York Post,* March 13, 2018, https://nypost.com/2018/03/13/ex-cuomo-aide-convicted-on-corruption-charges/.

110 Thomas D. Elias, "California state government awash in corruption, conflict of interest: Thomas Elias," *Los Angeles Daily News,* August 4, 2014, http://www.dailynews.com/opinion/20140804/california-state-government-awash-in-corruption-conflict-of-interest-thomas-elias.

111 The entire quote is, "Nearly all men can stand adversity but if you want to test a man's character give him power." "Abraham Lincoln Quotes," *BrainyQuote,* accessed January 16, 2018, https://www.brainyquote.com/quotes/quotes/a/abrahamlin101343.html.

112 "Benjamin Franklin: Founding Father Quote," *Founding Father Quotes,* accessed January 16, 2018, http://www.foundingfatherquotes.com/quote/652.

113 "From John Adams to Massachusetts Militia, 11 October 1798." *National Archives, Founders Online,* accessed January 16, 2018, https://founders.archives.gov/documents/Adams/99-02-02-3102.

[114] *The Advertiser* (1748), *Wikiquotes*, accessed January 16, 2018, https://en.wikiquote.org/wiki/Samuel_Adams.

[115] "Easing Rules on Lobbyists a Bad Idea" (Editorial), *Lexington Herald Leader*, September 27, 2015, http://www.kentucky.com/opinion/editorials/article42625509.html.

[116] Jeremy Adam Smith and Pamela Paxton, "America's Trust Fall," *Greater Good: The Science of a Meaningful Life*, September 1, 2008, http://greatergood.berkeley.edu/article/item/americas_trust_fall.

[117] Melanie Mason, "State legislators approve $52-billion transportation plan to repair California's ailing roads," *Los Angeles Times,* April 6, 2017, http://www.latimes.com/politics/essential/la-pol-ca-essential-politics-updates-in-a-squeaker-vote-assembly-approves-1491543684-htmlstory.html.

[118] Matt DeRienzo, "Political Corruption in Connecticut: Corrupticut Abides," *Connecticut Magazine,* June 1, 2013, http://www.connecticutmag.com/connecticut-magazine/political-corruption-in-connecticut-corrupticut-abides/article_59560325-1434-52f9-a0bc-8871387307e6.html.

[119] "Still, only a handful of the more than 14,000 suspected lobbying violations referred to authorities have been singled out for possible prosecution." Marcus E. Howard, "Penalty against lobbying firm sends message to an industry unfamiliar with prosecution," *Los Angeles Times*, November 30, 2015, http://www.latimes.com/nation/politics/la-na-lobbying-enforcement-20151130-story.html.

[120] Bill Ruthhart, "Five more lobbying violations tied to Emanuel personal emails," *Chicago Tribune,* July 19, 2017, http://www.chicagotribune.com/news/local/politics/ct-rahm-emanuel-chicago-lobbying-violations-met-0720-20170719-story.html.

[121] Jay Michael and Dan Walters, *The Third House,* 14.

122 "Legislator Gift Restrictions Overview," *NCSL*, September 9, 2016, http://www.ncsl.org/research/ethics/50-state-table-gift-laws.aspx.

123 Natalie O'Donnell Wood, "Gifts of Hospitality," *NCSL LegisBrief*, 22, no. 21 (June 2014), http://www.ncsl.org/research/ethics/gifts-of-hospitality.aspx.

124 "Honorarium Restrictions," *NCSL*, October 2015, http://www.ncsl.org/research/ethics/50-state-chart-honorarium-restrictions.aspx.

125 Texas Government Code § 305.024, .025(1), (2), (6) (2017).

126 "Limits on Campaign Contributions during the Legislative Session," *NCSL*, December 6, 2011, http://www.ncsl.org/research/elections-and-campaigns/limits-on-contributions-during-session.aspx.

127 Texas Government Code § 305.028 (2016); Revised Code of Washington 42.17A.655(2)(b) (2016).

128 65 Pennsylvania Consolidated Statutes § 13A07(f)(ix) (2016).

129 Carol A. Arscott and Patrick E. Gonzales, "Rules to Live by for Surviving in Annapolis," *The Baltimore Sun*, July 21, 2000, http://articles.baltimoresun.com/2000-07-21/news/0007210090_1_annapolis-lobbyist-lobbying.

130 California Government Code § 86205(e) (2015).

131 "Code of Conduct," *California Institute of Government Advocates*, accessed January 16, 2018, http://californiaiga.org/?page_id=30.

132 Benjamin Weiser, "Former Hospital Chief Convicted of Offering Bribes to Albany Legislators," *The New York Times*, September 11, 2011, http://www.nytimes.com/2011/09/13/nyregion/rosen-ex-hospital-chief-convicted-of-trying-to-bribe-assemblymen.html.

[133] "Specifically, from February 2010 through April 2011, DeBaggis caused State Street to pay $160,000 to Mohamed Noure Alo ('Alo') in purported lobbying fees, a substantial portion of which actually operated as kickbacks to Ahmad. In addition, DeBaggis, aided by Robert B. Crowe ('Crowe'), a State Street lobbyist, arranged for at least $60,000 in political contributions to the Treasurer's election campaign." "State Street Bank and Trust Company," *U.S. Securities and Exchange Commission*, January 14, 2016, https://www.sec.gov/litigation/admin/2016/34-76905.pdf.

[134] Washington, D.C. litigator, e-mail communication with author, February 24, 2017.

[135] Michael P. Kearns, "Another Voice: Term limits for state officials reduce corruption," *The Buffalo News*, May 21, 2016, http://buffalonews.com/2016/05/21/another-voice-term-limits-for-state-officials--reduce-corruption/.

[136] Nick Tomboulides, "Myth-Busting 101. Do Lobbyists Love Term Limits?," *U.S. Term Limits*, February 20, 2014, https://www.termlimits.com/myth-busting-101-lobbyists-love-term-limits/.

[137] Beth L. Leech, *Lobbyists at Work* (New York: Apress, 2013). Kindle edition.

[138] Larry Mankinson, *Speaking Freely: Washington Insiders Talk About Money in Politics*, 2nd ed. (Washington, D.C.: Center for Responsive Politics, 2003), 84.

[139] "Unruh Noted for Way With Words," *Los Angeles Times*, August 5, 1987, http://articles.latimes.com/keyword/jesse-m-unruh/recent/2.

[140] Most research on lobbying and campaign contributions is done at the federal level. In this chapter, research done in Washington, D.C., I extrapolate to the state level, and differences between the federal and state levels are noted when appropriate.

[141] Edwin Bender, "Evidencing a Republican Form of Government: The Influence of Campaign Money on State-Level Elections," *Montana Law Review*, 74, no. 1 (2013): 165, http://scholarship.law.umt.edu/mlr/vol74/iss1/8/.

[142] *Lobbyists at Work.*

[143] In-house lobbyist and former legislative staff, e-mail communication with author, October 6, 2017.

[144] Campaign consultant, e-mail communication with author, March 7, 2017.

[145] Endogeneity is, "A change or variable that arises from within a model or system. For example, a change in customer preferences from high fat foods to low fat options is an endogenous change that affects the marketing model for certain industries." *Business Dictionary,* accessed March 10, 2017, http://www. businessdictionary.com/definition/endogeneity.html.

[146] John Samples, *The Fallacy of Campaign Finance Reform* (Chicago: University of Chicago Press, 2006), 90.

[147] Alan Rosenthal, *Engines of Democracy* (Washington, D.C.: CQ Press, 2009), 166.

[148] *Speaking Freely*, 44.

[149] *Engines of Democracy*, 169-170.

[150] *Speaking Freely*, 42.

[151] *Citizen's Handbook to Influencing Elected Officials*, 31.

[152] Campaign manager, e-mail communication with author, March 7, 2017.

[153] Campaign manager, e-mail communication with author, March 7, 2017.

154 Lynda W. Powell, "The Influence Of Campaign Contributions On The Legislative Process," *Duke Journal of Constitutional Law and Public Policy* 9, no. 1 (2014), http://scholarship.law.duke.edu/cgi/viewcontent.cgi?article=1088&context=djclpp.

155 John Schwarz, "'Yes, We're Corrupt' A List of Politicians Admitting that Money Controls Politics," *The Intercept*, July 30, 2015, https://theintercept.com/2015/07/30/politicians-admitting-obvious-fact-money-affects-vote/.

156 Campaign consultant, e-mail communication with author, March 7, 2017.

157 Cenk Uygur, "TYT Interviews." YouTube video. 36:47. Uploaded July 11, 2017. https://www.youtube.com/watch?v=4FUcp4gq-zI. The particular comment can be found at the 9:51 point in the video.

158 Political campaign manager, email communication with author, March 7, 2017.

159 *Engines of Democracy*, 167.

160 *The Lobbying Handbook*, 703.

161 John Schwarz, "'Yes, We're Corrupt' A List of Politicians Admitting that Money Controls Politics."

162 Don Wolfensberger, "Factions and the Public Interest: Federalist No. 10 in 2001," *The Wilson Center*, May 18, 2001, https://www.wilsoncenter.org/sites/default/files/lobbyintro.pdf.

163 Lyndon B. Johnson, *Wikiquote*, accessed April 20, 2017, https://en.wikiquote.org/wiki/J._Edgar_Hoover; originally quoted in *The New York Times*, October 31, 1971.

164 I just don't remember if I picked up this phrasing from someone else or it's original to me. I can find no cite for it on the Internet. If you wrote it just tell me and I'll include the proper cite in the next edition of this book.

165 Contract lobbyist, e-mail communication
with author, October 2, 2017.

166 Rep. Julio Robaina made this comment to seminar attendees
at the conclusion of my presentation to the 2005 National
Convention of the National Association of Commission on
the Status of Women, Miami Beach, FL, July 16, 2005.

167 "Rubio Resigns from Senate," *The Foothills Sun-
Gazette*, February 27, 2013: A1, http://www.
thesungazette.com/?s=Rubio+resigns+from+Senate.

168 Chris Glorioso, "I-Team: New Jersey Lawmakers Have
Staffers Cast Their Votes," *NBC News: 4 New York*,
September 30, 2014, http://www.nbcnewyork.com/news/
local/Ghost-Voting-New-Jersey-Legislature-State-Senator-
Vote-Absent-277488441.html. However, "Official state
Senate rules clearly state that 'no Senator's vote shall be
recorded unless the Senator is present in the Chamber.'"

169 I discuss only the types of staffs with which I have worked.
However, NCSL lists more staff types including: *Clerks and
Secretaries, Fiscal Offices, Information Officers, Information
Technology, Leadership Staff, Legislative Staff Coordinating
Committee, Program Evaluation, Research Librarians, Research,
Editorial, Legal and Committee Staff, Services and Security.*
"Legislative Staff Services," *NCSL*, accessed February 27, 2017,
http://www.ncsl.org/legislators-staff/legislative-staff.aspx.

170 In-house lobbyist, personal communication with author, August 2010.

171 Megan Schrader, "Bipartisan sentiment quickly forgotten
as dozens of bills headed to kill committees in Colorado
Legislature," *The Gazette*, January 19, 2016, http://gazette.
com/bipartisan-sentiment-quickly-forgotten-as-dozens-
of-bills-headed-to-kill-committees-in-colorado-legislature/
article/1568169.

172 David Ash, former staff for Florida Senator Al Lawson, e-mail communication with author, June 2010.

173 "Running the traps" means checking for support and opposition. "In politics, however, one colorful slang phrase, used frequently by insiders, rarely sees the light of print: run the traps. It has a general meaning of 'survey those in the know...'" "On Language; Running the Traps RUNNING ON EMPTY," *The New York Times*, December 6, 1987, http://www.nytimes.com/1987/12/06/magazine/on-language-running-the-traps-running-on-empty.html.

174 *The Lobbying Handbook*, 731.

175 Lynn R. Muchmore and Thad L. Beyle, eds., *Being Governor: The View from the Office* (Durham, NC: Duke University Press, 1983), 126.

176 "A Company's Basic Guide to Lobbying in Florida," *Carlton Fields Jorden Burt, P.A.*, July 24, 2012, https://www.carltonfields.com/a-companys-basic-guide-to-lobbying-in-florida/.

177 Public employee union lobbyist, personal conversation with author, September 14, 2015.

178 "State Budget Procedures," *NCSL*, June 2017, http://www.ncsl.org/research/fiscal-policy/state-budget-procedures.aspx.

179 Abby Goodnough, "Vermont Exercising Option to Balance the Budget," *The New York Times*, April 23, 2011, http://www.nytimes.com/2011/04/24/us/24vermont.html.

180 Alana Semuels, "The Folly of State-Level Tax Cuts," *The Atlantic*, March 10, 2016, https://www.theatlantic.com/business/archive/2016/03/state-budget-crisis/473157/.

181 "Groups Praise Governor and Legislature for Increasing Farmland Protection Funding in State Budget," *Scenic*

Hudson, April 2, 2015, http://www.scenichudson.org/
news/release/groups-praise-Governor-and-legislature-
increasing-farmland-protection-funding-state.

[182] Dina Berliner, "Senate approves bill defunding
Planned Parenthood," *Columbus Dispatch*, Oct 21,
2015, http://www.dispatch.com/content/stories/
local/2015/10/21/planned-parenthood-funding.html.

[183] "Jacob Lew quotes," *BrainyQuote*, accessed February
22, 2018, https://www.brainyquote.com/quotes/jacob_
lew_442942. Lew was former U.S. Treasury Secretary.

[184] Greg A. Rowe, "Keeping the Courts Funded: Recommendations
on How Courts Can Avoid the Budget Axe," *Executive Session
for State Court Leaders in the 21st Century* (Harvard University/
National Center for State Courts), (circa 2012), http://www.sji.
gov/wp/wp-content/uploads/Keeping_Courts_Funded.pdf.

[185] Scott Jaschick, "Defunding Diversity," *Inside Higher
Ed*, April 22, 2016, https://www.insidehighered.com/
news/2016/04/22/both-Houses-tennessee-legislature-
vote-bar-use-state-funds-university-diversity.

[186] *Ivie v. Hickman*, Utah Court of Appeals, No. 20040071-
CA. December 16, 2004, http://caselaw.findlaw.
com/ut-court-of-appeals/1129269.html.

[187] Justin W. Evans and Mark C. Bannister, *The Meaning
and Purposes of State Constitutional Single Subject Rules: A
Survey of States and the Indiana Example*, 49 Val. U. L. Rev.
87 (2015), http://scholar.valpo.edu/vulr/vol49/iss1/10.

[188] Ronald K. Snell, "State Constitutional and Statutory
Requirements for Balanced Budgets," *NCSL*, accessed
June 28, 2017, http://www.ncsl.org/research/fiscal-policy/
state-constitutional-and-statutory-requirements-fo.aspx.

189 Katelyn Tye, "Halfway into fiscal year, Illinois still
operates without a budget," *The Council of State
Governments*, January 2016, http://www.csgmidwest.
org/policyresearch/0116-states-no-budget.aspx.

190 *The Lobbying Handbook*, 678.

191 Geoffrey Gitomer, "'Why They Buy' an answer
every sales person needs," *Buy Gitomer*, accessed
March 2, 2017, https://www.gitomer.com/
why-they-buy-an-answer-every-salesperson-needs-2/.

192 Debra Borchardt, "1 Billion in Marijuana Taxes is Addictive to
State Governors," *Forbes*, April 11, 2017, https://www.forbes.
com/sites/debraborchardt/2017/04/11/1-billion-in-marijuana-
taxes-is-addicting-to-state-Governors/#7c1a325e2c3b.

193 "Position on the Legalization of Marijuana,"
Massachusetts Chiefs of Police Association, July 2016,
https://www.masschiefs.org/files-downloads/
marijuana-updates/958-mass-chiefs-position-paper-pdf/file.

194 "Joint Statement from the International Association of Chiefs
of Police and the National Sheriffs Association on California's
Proposition 19," accessed October 11, 2017, http://www.
theiacp.org/portals/0/pdfs/IACP-NSAProp19Statement.pdf.

195 Jeffrey Gitomer, "People don't like to be sold-but they
love to buy," *BuyGitomer*, accessed March 2, 2017,
http://insightsquared.com/2013/06/20-great-quotes-
and-pearls-of-wisdom-from-jeffrey-gitomer/.

196 Blue state Senator, personal communication
with author, October 16, 2017.

197 Kirsten Weir, "Marijuana and the developing brain," *American
Psychological Association*, November 2015, Vol 46, No. 10, http://
www.apa.org/monitor/2015/11/marijuana-brain.aspx.

198 Blue state House member, personal communication with author, October 16, 2017.

199 G. Michael Dobbs, "Opinion: Why does the Conference Committee meet in secret?" *Springfield Magazine*, July 20, 2017, http://remindermagazines. com/springfield/articles/opinion_why_does_t/.

200 "Conference Committees," *NCSL*, accessed November 30, 2017, http://www.ncsl.org/documents/legismgt/ILP/96Tab4Pt3.pdf.

201 In-house lobbyist, e-mail communication with author, July 26, 2014.

202 Peter Noel Murray, "How Emotions Influence What We Buy," *Psychology Today*, February 26, 2013, https://www. psychologytoday.com/blog/inside-the-consumer-mind/201302/ how-emotions-influence-what-we-buy.

203 Briana Bierschbach, "The high cost of being a Minnesota legislator," *MinnPost*, July 16, 2015, https://www.minnpost.com/ politics-policy/2015/07/high-cost-being-minnesota-legislator.

204 Briana Bierschbach, "The high cost."

205 Alan Greenblatt, "Low Pay and Time Away Drive Some Lawmakers to Call It Quits," *Governing*, February 2017, http://www.governing.com/topics/ mgmt/gov-legislative-pay-salaries.html.

206 "[W]here the *whole* power of one department is exercised by the same hands which possess the *whole* power of another department, the fundamental principles of a free constitution, are subverted." (emphasis in original) James Madison, *Federalist, no. 10*, January 30, 1788, *The University of Chicago Press*, accessed November 27, 2017, http://press-pubs.uchicago.edu/founders/documents/v1ch10s14.html.

207 "Governors' Powers and Authority: Overview," *National Governors Association*, 2015, http://www.nga.org/cms/home/management-resources/Governors-powers-and-authority.html.

208 The ninety percent figure is *my extrapolation* to the state level of federal administrative rule promulgations. I have no state data to cite. "In 2015, 114 laws were enacted by Congress during the calendar year, while 3,410 rules were issued by agencies. Thus, 30 rules were issued for every law enacted last year." Clyde Wayne Crews, Jr., "Ten Thousand Commandments: An Annual Snapshot of the Federal Regulatory State, 2016 Edition," *Competitive Enterprise Institute*, January 5, 2017, https://cei.org/sites/default/files/WayneCrews-TenThousandCommandments2016-May42016.pdf.

209 W. L. Beale, "Power of the Governor: Did the Court Unconstitutionally Tell The Governor to Shut Up?," *Baylor Law Review*, April 5, 2010, www.bayor.edu/content/services/document.php/11697.pdf.

210 Kurt Erickson, "AFSCME raises concerns about National Guard use," *Herald & Review*, July 28, 2015, http://herald-review.com/news/state-and-regional/govt-and-politics/afscme-raises-concerns-about-national-guard-use/article_2f0352e0-1b40-5026-a9ae-b2b2b26539ec.html.

211 Rick Levanthal, "West Virginia calls in National Guard to tackle opioid crisis," *Fox News*, February 9, 2018, http://www.foxnews.com/health/2018/02/09/west-virginia-calls-in-national-guard-to-tackle-opioid-crisis.html.

212 Antonio Olivo, "Deployed by Gov. Rick Perry, National Guard adjusts to its new role on the Texas border," *The Washington Post*, September 1, 2014, https://www.washingtonpost.com/national/deployed-by-gov-rick-perry-national-guard-adjusts-to-its-new-role-on-the-texas-border/2014/09/01/24968056-2f90-11e4-994d-202962a9150c_story.html?utm_term=.f8af1cee46b0.

213 "Although I do not believe that government is ill-intentioned, I strongly believe in less government. I vetoed 750 bills as Governor because I abhor the government spending money on programs that show no improvement in our lives and criminalize actions that do not warrant criminalization." Charles Aull, "Did Gary Johnson issue 750 vetoes as Governor of New Mexico?" *Ballotpedia, Verbatim fact check,* January 27, 2016, https:// ballotpedia.org/Verbatim_fact_check:_Did_Gary_Johnson_ issue_750_vetoes_as_Governor_of_New_Mexico%3F.

214 John Myers, "Political Roadmap: There's a reason why Jerry Brown signs so many bills," *Los Angeles Times,* October 2, 2016, http://www.latimes.com/politics/la-pol-sac-roadmap-jerry-brown-signs-bills-20161002-snap-story.html.

215 Governors' Powers and Authority: Overview.

216 "Gubernatorial Veto Authority with Respect to Major Budget Bill(s): Legislative Budget Procedures: Enactment of the Budget," Table 6-3: Governors' Veto Power Regarding Appropriations Legislation, *NCSL,* December, 2008, http://www.ncsl.org/research/fiscal-policy/ gubernatorial-veto-authority-with-respect-to-major.aspx.

217 "General Legislative Procedures," *NCSL,* accessed January 5, 2017, http://www.ncsl.org/ documents/legismgt/ilp/98tab6pt3.pdf.

218 Bill Kaczor, "Florida lawmakers override 8 Crist vetoes," *Deseret News,* November 16, 2010, http:// www.deseretnews.com/article/700082591/Florida-lawmakers-override-8-Crist-vetoes.html?pg=all.

219 David Siders and Jim Miller, "Override Jerry Brown's veto? Not likely to happen," *The Sacramento Bee,* September 22, 2016, http://www.sacbee.com/news/politics-government/capitol-alert/article103302897.html.

220 Ovetta Wiggins and Josh Hicks, "Hogan vetoes six bills, setting stage for another override battle," *The Washington Post*, May 27, 2016, https://www.washingtonpost.com/local/md-politics/hogan-vetoes-six-bills-setting-stage-for-another-override-battle/2016/05/27/c2312b90-228c-11e6-8690-f14ca9de2972_story.html?utm_term=.9aefd389c8a4.

221 "Local Lawyers React to Cuomo's Veto of Indigent Defense Bill," *Fox News 28,* January 2, 2017, http://www.wwnytv.com/story/34167615/local-lawyers-react-to-cuomos-veto-of-indigent-defense-bill.

222 Randy Ludlow, "Gov. John Kasich vetoes Heartbeat Bill, signs 20-week abortion ban," *Columbus Dispatch*, December 14, 2016, http://www.dispatch.com/content/stories/local/2016/12/13/John-Kasich-acts-on-abortion-bills.html.

223 Zoe Balaconis, "Georgia Governor Will Veto LGBT Bill, Proving Just How Powerful Public Outcry Can Be," *romper.com*, March 28, 2016, https://www.romper.com/p/georgia-Governor--veto-lgbt-bill-proving-just-how-powerful-public-outcry-can-be-7851.

224 Former gubernatorial staff member, e-mail communication with author, May 24, 2017.

225 Judson Berger, "West Virginia Governor displays bull dung, as budget metaphor—yes, this really happened," *Fox News Politics*, April 14, 2017, http://www.foxnews.com/politics/2017/04/14/west-virginia-Governor-displays-bull-dung-as-budget-metaphor-yes-this-really-happened.html.

226 Former gubernatorial staff, e-mail communication with author, May 24, 2017.

227 Thomas Jefferson to the Abbé Arnoux, "The Founders' Constitution, Volume 5, Amendment VII, Document 13," *The*

University of Chicago, accessed April 13, 2017, http://press-pubs.uchicago.edu/founders/documents/amendVIIs13.html.

228 Dwight Waldo, *The Administrative State* (1948). This book has been republished many times since first written. I refer the edition by Transaction Publishers: New Brunswick, 2007, 90. See also, "The Administrative State," *Wikipedia,* accessed September 14, 2015, https://en.wikipedia.org/wiki/The_Administrative_State.

229 Paul R. Verkuil, "The Purposes and Limits of Independent Agencies," *Duke Law Journal,* 1988, http://scholarship.law.duke.edu/cgi/viewcontent.cgi?article=3032&context=dlj.

230 Phillip Hamburger, *The Administrative Threat,* Encounter Intelligence, May 2, 2017, Kindle edition.

231 The term "program hoarders" was given to me by a Deloitte consultant with extensive experience working with government; he used this pithy insightful term in our conversation circa 2014.

232 William Sanjour, "Designed to Fail: Why Regulatory Agencies Don't Work," *Independent Science News,* May 1, 2012, https://www.independentsciencenews.org/health/designed-to-fail-why-regulatory-agencies-dont-work/.

233 Designed to Fail.

234 5 U.S. Code 551 (4), *Cornell Legal Information Institute,* accessed January 17, 2017, https://www.law.cornell.edu/uscode/text/5/551.

235 Roni A. Elias, "The Legislative History of the Administrative Procedure Act," *27 Fordham Envtl. L. Rev. 207* (2016), http://commons.law.famu.edu/cgi/viewcontent.cgi?article=1012&context=studentworks.

236 "State-Level Administrative Law," *Justicia,* accessed March 14, 2017, https://www.justia.com/administrative-law/state-level-administrative-law/.

237   "State Administrative Procedure Act, Revised
      Model," *Uniform Law Commission*, accessed
      March 15, 2017, http://www.uniformlaws.org/Act.
      aspx?title=StateAdministrativeProcedureAct,Revised Model

238   *The Administrative Threat.*

239   *Heckler v. Chaney*, 470 U.S. 821-831 (1985).

240   *Sierra Club, Petitioner, v. Lee M. Thomas, Administrator,
      Environmental Protection Agency et al., National Coal
      Association, Intervenors,* 828 F.2d 783, 793 (United States
      Court of Appeals, District of Columbia Circuit) (1987).

241   Cornelius M. Kerwin, *Rulemaking How Government
      Agencies Write Law and Make Policy,* 3rd edition
      (CQ Press: Washington, D.C., 2003), 52-58.

242   *Rulemaking How Government Agencies
      Write Law and Make Policy,* 52.

243   *The Administrative Threat.*

244   Ronald Pestritto, "The Birth of the Administrative State:
      Where It Came From and What It Means for Limited
      Government," *The Heritage Foundation*, November 20, 2007,
      http://www.heritage.org/political-process/report/the-birth-the-
      administrative-state-where-it-came-and-what-it-means-limited.

245   I borrowed this phrase to apply to executive agencies from
      Malcolm Feeley, *The Process Is the Punishment: Handling Cases in a
      Lower Criminal Court*, (Russel Sage Foundation: New York 1979).

246   Joseph A. McCartin, "Convenient Scapegoat:
      Public Workers under Assault," *Dissent,* Spring
      2011, https://www.dissentmagazine.org/article/
      convenient-scapegoat-public-workers-under-assault.

INDEX